Winning on Betfair

FOR

DUMMIES

by Jack Houghton

WILEY

Wiley Publishing, Inc.

Winning on Betfair For Dummies®

Published by
John Wiley & Sons, Ltd
The Atrium
Southern Gate
Chichester
West Sussex
PO19 8SQ
England

E-mail (for orders and customer service enquires): cs-books@wiley.co.uk

Visit our Home Page on www.wileyeurope.com

Copyright © 2006 John Wiley & Sons, Ltd, Chichester, West Sussex, England

Published by John Wiley & Sons, Ltd, Chichester, West Sussex

Wiley also publishes its books in a variety of electronic formats. Some content that appears in print may not be available in electronic books.

British Library Cataloguing in Publication Data: A catalogue record for this book is available from the British Library.

ISBN-10: 0-470-02856-4 (PB)

ISBN-13: 978-0-470-02856-8 (PB)

Printed and bound in Great Britain by Cox & Wyman Ltd, Reading, Berkshire.

10 9 8 7 6 5 4 3 2 1

WILEY

About the Author

Jack Houghton is the Head of Horseracing Communications at Betfair. He has been a life-long punter and jumped at the chance to work at Betfair when offered a job there in 2004.

He also works as a freelance journalist writing about horseracing and betting and won the Martin Wills Award for racing journalism in 2002.

Author's Acknowledgements

I'd like to thank my dad. Without him I wouldn't have gone racing for the first time and been introduced to the wonderfully varied and exciting world that is horseracing and betting. I should probably thank my mum as well. She fed me when I was growing up (and still does now occasionally) and will be annoyed if dad gets a mention and she doesn't.

Betfair is the best company in the world to work for and thanks should go to the various people that make the place what it is. It was a company founded on an idea that punters deserved a fairer deal and that attitude still pervades. I've learnt so much here and continue to learn from those I work with every day.

Special mention should go at this point to Tom Large who has driven the Dummies Project here at Betfair. He sorted out all the necessary things that go into writing a book that I was too lazy to do myself. The book would not have been completed without him.

Martin Tribe and the team at Wiley deserve thanks for all the help and encouragement they gave this rookie book-writer.

Oh, and my best friends, most of all Charlotte, for putting up with me.

Publisher's Acknowledgements

We're proud of this book; please send us your comments through our Dummies online registration form located at www.dummies.com/register/.

Some of the people who helped bring this book to market include the following:

Acquisitions, Editorial, and Media Development

Executive Project Editor: Martin Tribe

Content Editor: Simon Bell

Commissioning Editor: Alison Yates

Development Editor: Kelly Ewing

Copy Editor: Andrew Finch

Proofreader: Christine Lea

Technical Editor: Tom Large

Executive Editor: Jason Dunne

Cover Photo: Jupiter Images/ Image Source

Cartoons: Rich Tennant, www.the5thwave.com

Production

Project Coordinator: Maridee Ennis, Jennifer Theriot

Layout and Graphics: Carl Byers, Joyce Haughey, Stephanie D. Jumper, Heather Ryan

Proofreaders: Susan Moritz, Dwight Ramsey, Brian H. Walls

Indexer: TECHBOOKS Production Services

Publishing and Editorial for Consumer Dummies

   Diane Graves Steele, Vice President and Publisher, Consumer Dummies

   Joyce Pepple, Acquisitions Director, Consumer Dummies

   Kristin A. Cocks, Product Development Director, Consumer Dummies

   Michael Spring, Vice President and Publisher, Travel

   Kelly Regan, Editorial Director, Travel

Publishing for Technology Dummies

   Andy Cummings, Vice President and Publisher, Dummies Technology/ General User

Composition Services

   Gerry Fahey, Vice President of Production Services

   Debbie Stailey, Director of Composition Services

Contents at a Glance

• •

Table of Contents

● ●

Introduction

● ●

*N*o one knows when the first bet was placed, except that it was a long time ago. Archaeologists and anthropologists have plenty to occupy their time and I'm guessing that this matter just hasn't seemed important up to now. However, I'd like to urge them to turn their attentions to this important issue. When was the momentous point in human history where one cave dweller turned to another and uttered 'I bet you that. . .?'

Whenever history's first bet was made, it started off a chain of events making betting and gambling a central part of many cultures and, by the start of the 21st Century, a booming industry worth many billions of pounds.

Within the betting industry are all types of characters – from state-run betting outlets to massive corporations quoted on stock exchanges to small independent operators. And all these service the betting and gambling needs of an insatiable public.

What's interesting in this short history is that betting soon turned from something that occurred between two individuals to something that occurred between an individual and a betting organisation. And for many years that was the accepted norm.

Then, in June 2000, Betfair was born, and the story turned full circle. Although still betting through an organisation, Betfair odds are set by other individuals. Pure, unadulterated, person-to-person betting.

About This Book

This book specifically covers what Betfair is and how you can go about betting, and winning, on it.

I cover everything from the most basic areas – what Betfair is, how you open an account, how you place your first bet – to more advanced betting techniques and strategies that help you in your quest for profit.

I am clearly a died-in-the-wool Betfair fan but I've tried to be objective in writing this book. Lots of winning strategies involve using other forms of betting and I've highlighted this where relevant.

Conventions Used in This Book

The way that this book is put together has been planned to entertain and inform you. You'll find a lot of detail and a whole host of icons that explain different bits and pieces along the way.

Sidebars (text enclosed in a shaded grey box) are pieces of information that are interesting but not central to the story. You can skip them altogether, save them for later, or read them with the general text. The same is true for text next to the Technical Stuff icon. This icon is there for your information, and gives you the inner detail. But the material isn't necessary for your understanding of the topic. Again, skip it if you want. This isn't homework, and no one will know.

Foolish Assumptions

I had to make some assumptions about the kind of person who'd want to read this book. As a starting point, I pinned up the names of five people who I knew and tried to write a book that would be useful to them. I hope you feel that you are coming at this book from a similar background to at least one of them:

- ✔ My dad loves gambling. In an effort to support the chosen career of his son, he uses Betfair. Unfortunately he doesn't use computers and so instructs my mum what bets he wants. She's getting quite good at placing the bets now, but still occasionally calls up on a Saturday morning for advice. Don't get me wrong, I love receiving calls from my mum, but I'm not a morning person and I hope this book will afford me a couple of extra hours sleep.

- ✔ A friend of mine lives abroad and bets a lot on horseracing with the state-run pool betting they have there. He's actually pretty good at picking winners, but, unfortunately, the profit margins that are built in to the pool he bets with means he will never make a profit with them in the long-run. He could be a winner if he started using Betfair and I hope this book persuades him to make the switch.

- ✔ Another friend of mine is passionate about sport and uses online fixed-odds bookmakers to place the odd bet. He's had a look at Betfair a few times but finds it a bit overwhelming and involved when all he wants to do is place the odd bet. But I know he'd love it when he got into it, and so I hope the book gives him the impetus to give Betfair a go.

> ✔ An ex-colleague has used Betfair and other book-
> makers for a while, playing around with different
> strategies. He's at the point where he wants to be
> more serious about it and so I hope this book helps
> him get his head around some of the more advanced
> approaches that he could be using.
>
> ✔ The distant relative I keep bumping into who always
> asks me what I do and then looks slightly perplexed
> when I explain. Lots of people I meet don't want to
> bet, but are interested in Betfair as a company. This
> book should give those people a good overview of
> what Betfair is all about.

How This Book Is Organised

You can read this book from beginning to end or jump
from topic to topic. To make getting around the book,
and winning on Betfair, easier I've divided the book into
four parts.

Part 1: Starting Out

This is all about getting your head around what Betfair
is and how the concept works. I cover how to open an
account and manage it, and how to decide what kind of
things you want to bet on.

Part II: Let's Get Betting

This is where things start for real. In this section you'll
place your first bet, get your head around the different
types of bet you can choose and get a grip on the

mathematics behind betting. You'll also try out in-play betting – one of the things that makes Betfair completely different from other betting options out there.

Part III: Getting Serious

If you intend having more than the occasional bet and want to start thinking about making consistent profits on Betfair, this section is for you. It covers some of the low risk betting strategies that can be utilised to make money, explains how you might go about automating some of your betting and talks about what it takes to make a living (or at least a good second living) from betting. There's also a chapter on problem gambling. If you feel that betting is starting to play an unhealthy part in your life, check out this chapter for where to look for help.

Part IV: The Part of Tens

This bit of the book gives you a whole load of useful and interesting information about your quest for profit. It includes advice on things to do and things to avoid and tells some stories from Betfair's short and colourful history.

Icons Used in This Book

Some sections in each chapter are more important than other bits and I have highlighted these for you – whether it's a particularly good piece of advice or something important to be aware of. Icons highlight which bits these are.

Certain things you discover on Betfair make your betting life easier. This icon highlights when I'm about to write something that you might find particularly useful in your betting.

 This icon highlights advice, but rather than things that make your life easier, this icon stresses things you should be aware of. It emphasises things that stop you making a mistake.

 More serious than Remember icons, Warnings draw your attention to things that could have a seriously negative affect on your bank balance!

 You can skip these bits, but they do assist you in understanding some of the more complex points and give you additional information.

Where to Go from Here

Log on to Betfair at www.betfair.com

And get going – it's as simple as that!

Part I
Starting Out

The 5th Wave

By Rich Tennant

©RICHTENNANT

"You don't find it a bit negative that you chose 'UNLUCKY1' for our Betfair password?"

In this part . . .

Here we cover all the basics: what Betfair is, why it's a good thing, what you need to get started, how to open and manage an account and how to decide what it is you want to bet on.

Chapter 1

What is Betfair?

● ●

In This Chapter

▶ Understanding the Betfair idea

▶ Realising the benefits of Betfair

● ●

Betfair is the world's leading online betting exchange –
www.betfair.com. It allows people with different
opinions on the likely outcome of an event to bet against
each other, thanks to the invention of some clever technology by a boffin called Andrew 'Bert' Black in the late
1990s.

But that's all you need to know about the technical side.
This chapter covers what Betfair is, how it works, and
why it's so popular.

Getting Your Head Around Betfair

I have sat through countless demonstrations at Betfair
headquarters where people try to explain what Betfair
is to slightly perplexed audiences. The demonstrator

usually starts by showing everyone the Betfair Homepage (www.betfair.com), selecting a sporting event to bet on, and then beginning an explanation of what the mass of moving numbers mean.

Around four years ago, I went to the Betfair Homepage for the first time and can still remember how confused and dazzled I felt – a bit like a learner driver having his first driving experience on a motorway. The homepage can seem exhaustively complex at first when all you want to do is have a bet, but when you get used to it, it's actually quite straightforward. I look at the homepage in more detail in Chapter 4.

The best way to understand Betfair is to forget about the Web site for the time being. You don't actually need it to understand what Betfair is all about.

Think of this example instead. You're in a bar with your friend, and there's a soccer match on television. AC Milan are playing Juventus. Your friend says to you, 'I bet you Juventus wins.' You disagree. So you offer your friend odds of 2.0 on Juventus winning (meaning he wins £1 from you for every £1 he stakes). He bets £20.

Despite being friends, you don't altogether trust each other to hold the money, so you agree that the barman holds the money until the match is over. Your friend gives the barman his £20 stake, and you give the barman the £20 of potential winnings.

If Juventus wins, the barman gives your friend all the money. If AC Milan wins or it's a draw, the barman gives you the money.

That's all Betfair is really – a barman in a global betting bar (see Figure 1-1), although Betfair isn't licensed to serve alcohol!

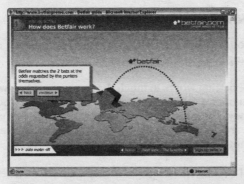

Figure 1-1: Betfair: a barman in a global betting village.

In my example, you have to be face to face with the person you disagree with to have the bet. With Betfair, you're matched up anonymously against people with different views from all over the world. If Margaret in South Africa thinks AC Milan will win, and Mike in Canada thinks they won't, Betfair holds the money until the result is known.

Revolutionising Betting

Opportunities for you to bet vary from country to country. I've heard that in some countries, betting is illegal. This piece of information upsets me, so I choose to believe that such places don't exist.

Before Betfair, there were two main outlets for you to bet on sports: pool-betting operators and fixed-odds bookmakers.

Pool betting operators

In countries where betting is legal, government run *pool betting* is often the main way of betting.

Pool betting works in much the same way as a sweepstake. A number of people bet on an event, creating a pool of money. The operator of the pool takes a cut (usually upwards of 20 per cent) and then gives out the rest of the money to the customers who chose the winning selection.

Pool betting has a couple of major disadvantages:

- The odds are completely reliant on how many other people choose the same outcome, and so you have no idea what odds you're going to get on the selection you're choosing.

- The transaction can't be changed and the pool closes when the contest starts, which means that you must place your bet before a contest starts and await your fate.

- Because the pool operator takes a large cut before giving out winnings, the odds you eventually get can be disappointing, especially on popular selections.

Fixed-odds bookmakers

In some countries, bookmakers are allowed to operate in this way. Bookmakers offer their own odds on any range of sporting contests. In some cases, you will be allowed to *take a price*, meaning that you know what odds your bet will be settled at if it wins.

But bookmakers have this advantage over pool-betting operators, the actual price you get has a profit margin built in on the side of the bookmaker. (See Chapter 6 for more on how bookmakers build in a profit margin.)

Enter Betfair

For many years, betting with pool operators and bookmakers were your only two options. Then, in the late 1990s, Andrew Black, or Bert as he is known, came up with the idea of using the stock exchange model to operate betting markets. This model means that customers can buy and sell, or *back* and *lay*, the outcomes of sporting events in much the same way that people buy and sell shares.

Revenge of the nerd

Andrew 'Bert' Black's background doesn't immediately suggest that he would become arguably one of the most successful Internet entrepreneurs.

Bert was the grandson of an inveterate anti-gambling campaigner. After being thrown out of university at the end of his first year, Bert had many jobs: a professional gambler; a professional bridge player; a derivatives trader; a golf caddie; and a software engineer. While in his last job at GCHQ (the top-secret UK government communications department), Bert began to work on the idea of the betting exchange.

Bert developed the idea into a working model and with his business partner, Edward Wray, launched Betfair in 2000. Just over five years later, the business now has nearly half a million customers, betting in 200 countries, in 17 languages, and 10 currencies.

Benefiting from the Exchange

The PR department at Betfair talks about lots of very honourable things including transparency, integrity, and honesty.

This is all very well, but I'm much more interested in what I get *out* of betting with Betfair. I'm going to tell you about four main benefits that Betfair offers over more traditional ways of betting. They are

- ✔ The confidence that you are getting better odds.
- ✔ The ability to back and lay.
- ✔ The ability to bet in-play.
- ✔ The knowledge that Betfair is not going to close your account down if you happen to win.

Better odds

You get better odds on Betfair because you are betting against individuals and not a bookmaker. Bookmakers have to make a profit because they have wages to pay, shops to run, and shareholders to satisfy. This means that every time a bookmaker offers you odds on something happening, a profit margin is built into those odds. I explain how this is done in Chapter 6.

On Betfair, you're matched up against an individual who disagrees with you. That person wants to win, but is less cautious in the odds they offer than a professional bookmaker and so doesn't build in a big profit margin.

A good example is betting on the outcome of the toss of a coin . If you toss a coin and ask a bookmaker to give you odds on the coin showing heads, you would expect him to say 2.0 (you make £5 profit for every £5 you stake). If he is following the exact probability of heads showing, that's what he would offer you (because there's a 50 per cent chance of it being heads). But if the bookmaker did that, he wouldn't make any profit, because in the long run you'd win half the time and the two of you would just keep handing £5 notes to each other.

Instead, the bookmaker offers you odds of 1.8. This means that if you bet £5 and won you would make £4 profit, but if you lost, you would lose £5. You would expect to win every other bet, but the bookmaker knows that in the long run, he will make money from you.

On Betfair, on the other hand, you're much more likely to get odds of 2.0, or at least very close, because it's just two people taking opposing views.

Sweeping statements are difficult to make about exactly how much better the prices are on Betfair compared to traditional bookmakers. Betfair's marketing literature talks about 'on average 20 per cent better odds.' This percentage is probably about right, but it depends greatly on what you're betting on.

A good general rule is to count the number of outcomes in a particular event and suppose 2 per cent an outcome. So if only two outcomes are possible, like a tennis match for example, the odds on Betfair would probably be around 4 per cent better on average than with a traditional bookmaker. In a race with 30 horses on the other hand, that figure could rise to as much 60 per cent.

Back and lay

Unlike a bookmaker, Betfair allows you to *lay* a selection (predict that it will not win) as well as *back* it to win. This ability is a key factor in you becoming a winning gambler. For example, you can study a contest for ages, understand it inside out, and identify a number of competitors that won't win, but can't necessarily say who will win. Being able to lay gives you an opportunity to bet in circumstances where betting wasn't available before.

1,900 per cent better odds

Occasionally, when betting, particularly on long shots, some massive odds are available on Betfair.

In January 2003, a horse called Gig Harbour was running at Lingfield Park racecourse. The bookies thought he had very little chance of winning and so they offered odds of 26.0 (meaning that the horse would be expected to win once in every 26 times the race took place).

On Betfair, a customer thought Gig Harbour had a chance and managed to back the horse at 500, because another customer was prepared to lay these odds, which were a massive 1,900 per cent better than the bookmaker's odds!

Unfortunately, this kind of thing doesn't happen everyday, but it's a good example of how individuals on Betfair often take much more aggressive positions than bookmakers and lay selections at much bigger odds than you can get elsewhere.

In financial markets, traders talk about operating on 'both sides of the market', meaning that someone is buying and selling. In this way, people can take part in trading and *arbitrage* – where low-risk profits are guaranteed by buying-low and selling-high (or the other way round). Being able to back as well as lay on Betfair allows you to do the same thing in betting markets (see Chapter 8).

The flexibility to back and lay opens up many more betting opportunities for you now than before.

In-play betting

Betfair has pioneered in-play betting. As the name suggests, *in-play betting* is betting while an event is in progress. Betfair offers a range of in-play opportunities – soccer, cricket, tennis, horse-racing, and more – allowing you to bet right up until the end of the contest.

In the case of horse-racing, you can bet right up until the first horse crosses the line. And if it's a photo finish, you can keep betting on which horse has won until the stewards make their decision. This is sometimes many minutes after the race has finished!

The ability to bet in-play is another key factor in you winning . You might fancy a tennis player to win a match but know that they can only win if they serve well – something that can't be guaranteed. Being able to bet in-play means that you can now watch a few service games and make a decision. If the player hasn't got their serving shoes on, you might decide to leave the bet well alone or even change your mind altogether and lay, rather than back the player.

A strange in-play story

At Southwell racecourse in January 2002, a horse called Family Business fell early in the race. A fast Betfair customer was able to lay the horse at 1,000 (the longest odds available on Betfair). Unfortunately for this layer, the other five horses also fell. The jockey remounted Family Business and went on to finish the race and win. Showing that there's no such thing as a certainty.

Winners always welcome

Bookmakers want to make money because it's how they make their living. They don't like you to consistently win money from them. Most bookmakers regularly review the accounts of all their customers and do one of two things: either start limiting the customer's bets or close the account down altogether.

Bookmakers are amazingly serious about this. A famous high street bookmaker once closed my account after I'd placed three winning bets with them in a month. Ironically, these bets were my only winning bets of the month – I'd placed a number of other bets with other bookmakers and lost far more than I'd won with this particular bookmaker. It just so happened that my only three winning bets were with this one operator.

Some people get very irate at the practice of bookmakers closing accounts down. They think it goes against the spirit of betting. After all, the argument goes, if bookmakers can't accept that you are going to win, they shouldn't be in the game.

I'm actually pretty relaxed about the practice. If I were a bookmaker, I'd do the same thing.

You do have a choice. On Betfair, accounts are never limited or closed just because you happen to be a winner.

Chapter 2

Starting Out with the Essentials

● ●

In This Chapter

▶ Lining up your computer equipment

▶ Setting up a Betfair account

▶ Making deposits and withdrawals

● ●

My ex-girlfriend's uncle liked to tell a story when he'd had a drink or two. The story was about a wannabee pole-vaulter who turned up at a track and field meeting with brand new shoes, a luminous coloured vest, and all other sorts of athletic equipment. Except for one thing – he didn't have the pole.

The uncle thought this story hilarious. I disagreed. I particularly disagreed the second, third, fourth, and fifth time around.

Despite the despair I felt each time the uncle leapt up to begin (the story was accompanied by various actions), I did gain a valuable lesson. Before starting on any activity, you need to have the essentials in place. Betfair is no exception to that rule.

To begin winning on Betfair, your essentials are a computer with an Internet connection, a Betfair account, and some money in that account.

Getting the Right Equipment

You can use Betfair on most computers (Macs or PCs) that have an Internet browser and an Internet connection.

Betfair has no set minimum hardware requirements such as memory or disk space. However, the faster your machine and the more free memory you have, the quicker Betfair will work. Winning on Betfair is sometimes about making split second decisions and a speedier set up helps.

Also, you can have more than one Web site open at a time with a better machine. If you're betting on a soccer match for example, you may want several different items to appear at once – Betfair; a sporting results service; a sports form guide; and an online radio station that is giving you a match commentary. A slower machine struggles to process information when you have more than one Web site running, which can be frustrating.

The type of Internet connection you have also affects how much you enjoy your Betfair experience. In theory, even the slowest dial-up connection allows you to use Betfair, but to get the most out of it, a faster connection, such as ISDN or broadband, is better. When using a dial-up connection, you may often find that odds have changed or that events have already started by the time you place your bets.

If you have any technical questions or issues, call the Betfair Helpdesk for advice.

Opening a Betfair Account

Before you begin to place bets, you need to open a Betfair account. Simply launch the Internet on your computer and go to www.betfair.com.

Click the Join Now link, and you see the New User Registration window (see Figure 2-1), where you're asked to fill in personal and account details. (The next two sections walk you through the details.)

Figure 2-1: Entering your personal details.

Knowing me, knowing you: Why Betfair wants to know you

You may get frustrated when you're asked to give information about yourself if all you want to do is have a bet!

Betfair, though, needs to know who you are. Are you over 18? Is the money you're gambling with yours?

Usually, Betfair can get all the information it needs from the details you complete when registering. But occasionally, if you're trading a lot of money through an account, Betfair asks you to complete a *Know Your Customer (KYC) check.* This check is very similar to checks done by banks.

To start with, this check involves confirming your name and address, your age, and your contact details using the Web site via a message board, e-mail, or telephone.

Next, you are asked to give proof of identification, address, and source of funds together with documentation.

If you're asked to complete a KYC check, Betfair will contact you by e-mail or post.

Personal details

Betfair needs to confirm your identity and how old you are. Fill in your title, name, and date of birth. Betfair is legally responsible if anyone under the age of 18 uses the site and so needs to do everything possible to make sure this doesn't happen, which is why the company asks for these details. (See 'Knowing me, knowing you: Why Betfair wants to know you' for more details.)

Key in your home address, e-mail address, and a telephone number so that Betfair can contact you if there is ever has a question about your account. At this stage, you can also choose whether you want to receive marketing materials from Betfair.

You can say no to companies who want to send you marketing materials. I get sent so much junk by post and e-mail these days that I certainly wish I'd been a little more selective over the boxes I ticked when filling in forms. However, the material that Betfair sends to its customers can be quite useful – TV schedules, statistics, articles – and when you're trying to win on Betfair, you don't want to put yourself at an information disadvantage compared with other customers. If, at a later date, you think the material is a load of rubbish, you can always opt not to receive any more by following a link at the bottom of the e-mails you are sent.

Lastly, in this section, key in any promotional or Refer And Earn code that you may have. (See 'Refer And Earn' below for more on this code.) When advertising, Betfair often offers free bets to new customers so that you can try the site without risking your money.

Refer And Earn

Betfair runs a scheme called Refer And Earn, which can be a useful way of supplementing your betting bank. The scheme asks you to get your friends to open an account using your unique Refer And Earn code. (Your code is in the My Account section on the Betfair homepage.)

When your friend opens an account and has a few bets, you both receive a free £20 bet. Then, after three months, depending on how much your friend bets, you both receive a reward. You receive additional rewards every three months for up to a year. If your friend is a particularly big bettor, you can receive more than £8,000 in that first year.

Make sure that you key in any promotional code correctly. All special offers are processed automatically, and the system finds it difficult to pick these up if you've entered something inaccurately.

After you have keyed in all your personal information on this screen, click Next. You now see a page to confirm your address details. If the details are correct, click Next again.

Account details

After you have filled in all your personal details (see above), you need to choose a Username and Password, which you'll use every time you access your account (see Figure 2-2). The Username and Password should be easy for you to remember, but not so easy that it could be guessed by anyone else.

Figure 2-2: Choosing your account details.

An easy way to lose money

I use the Internet for a lot of things – banking, shopping – as well as betting. When checking my credit-card statement one month, I noticed that I'd apparently spent more than £300 with an online bookshop.

After looking into it closely, I discovered that a disgruntled bank employee had gone into my account, recovered my Username and Password, and guessed that I might use the same combination elsewhere. The employee was right. Using different details with different companies takes only a little extra effort, but by using different combinations could save you a packet.

Choose a Username and a Password that is made up of both letters and numbers. Using characters like £, %, or * makes your Username and Password more secure.

You now answer just two security questions, which help to confirm your identity if you forget your Password, if you need to contact the Betfair Helpdesk and want them to change details on your account, or if you e-mail Betfair from a non-registered e-mail address. Just like your Username and Password, choose questions and answers that others can't guess easily.

Betfair never asks you for your Password or security questions by e-mail. If you receive an e-mail asking for this information, call Betfair at once.

Next, you're asked to retype a series of letters and numbers that appear in a box. The box is displayed in such a way that a computer hacker isn't able to read it, and which stops a hacker from copying your details and controlling your account.

Select your time zone (all event times are shown on the site in both your own time zone and also in local time), and the currency you'd like to use. You can set a limit on the amount of deposits you want to make to your account in any day or week.

This method is useful for setting limits if you're worried about spending more than you can afford on Betfair. You can change the amounts at a later date, but although decreases are done immediately, any increase takes 24 hours. If you feel you're gambling too much, see Chapter 12 for more information about what to do.

Finally, you're asked to confirm that you agree to the terms and conditions of Betfair and that you're over 18 years of age.

When this section is completed, click Next, and you see a page about funding your account. (See the next two sections, 'Depositing Money' and 'Withdrawing Money', for information on how to fund your account for the first time.)

Always make sure that you log out and close all windows when you leave your computer.

Depositing Money

At the end of the registration process (see 'Opening a Betfair Account' earlier in this chapter), you see a screen that says your account is open and ready to be funded. This screen gives you three main options:

✔ Fund using a credit or debit card

✔ Fund with a direct bank transfer

✔ Fund by other means

I'm going to assume that you're using a credit or debit card to fund your account (see Figure 2-3 below). Although you can deposit money in other ways, using a card is the cheapest and most convenient way to do so. If you can, forget the other methods.

Remember this book is about betting not banking. If you're unable to use a credit or debit card, go to http://payments.betfair.com to find information about alternative methods. Otherwise, call the Betfair Helpdesk for advice.

After you have selected the credit or debit card option, you're asked to enter your card details, including a Card Nickname. This nickname is how the card appears on your account so that if you register more than one card, you know which one is which.

Now enter the amount you want to deposit and the card security code (the last three digits on the back of the card, usually found above the signature strip) and then click Make Deposit.

A charge of 1.5 per cent is made on deposits when using some credit cards. If in doubt, call the Betfair Helpdesk to check.

After you've deposited money for the first time, your card details are stored on the system, making transactions much simpler in future.

To put more money in your account:

1. **Click the My Account link at the top of the Betfair homepage. The My Account area will popup.**

2. **Click Deposit Funds on the left-hand menu.**

3. **Enter the amount you want to deposit, your security code, and your account password.**

If you forget your password, click the Forgotten Your Password link just below the Login section of the Web site. Betfair guides you through a series of questions. When you've correctly answered the questions, you can set up a new password of your choice.

4. **Click Make Deposit.**

The money appears in your account at once.

Figure 2-3: Getting money into your account.

Withdrawing Money

If you have followed everything in this book carefully you will hopefully regularly win money from betting on Betfair! If so, from time to time you may want to withdraw money from your account to spend on other things.

To withdraw money from your account:

1. **From the Betfair homepage, click My Account at the top of the screen. The My Account area will popup.**

2. **Click Withdraw Funds on the left-hand menu.**

   You see a summary of all the credit and debit cards you have registered to an account.

3. **Enter the amount you want to withdraw and to which card the money should be credited.**

4. **Enter your account Password and then click Withdraw Funds.**

Although card deposits are usually instant, withdrawals can take two to five days to appear in your bank account.

Chapter 3

Managing Your Account

. . . .

In This Chapter

▶ Keeping an eye on your Betfair account

▶ Making it easier to get to the markets you want

▶ Exchanging ideas on the Betfair Forum

. . . .

I watch a lot of people using Betfair in the course of my work, and it's quite an enlightening experience. No two people are the same.

I was talking to someone the other day who has been a Betfair customer for over four years. To most people, he would seem like a fairly savvy user. He does lots of clever betting, such as trading and arbing. (I talk about trading in Chapter 8 and arbing in Chapter 9.) And he does them well – he's made a profit on Betfair every year that he's been a customer.

Yet, despite his obvious knowledge, I became increasingly frustrated by his long-winded way of doing everything. He made a note of everyone of his bets on a piece of paper (Betfair does this for you). He kept a running total of his profit and loss (Betfair does this for you). He took forever to navigate to the parts of the site he wanted even though he repeatedly went back to exactly the same places (Betfair can help you do this). All in all, I reckoned that he was spending at least 25 per cent more time doing things than is necessary.

In this chapter I go through a few things to make your life easier when using Betfair.

Working with My Account

If you want to do anything on Betfair that isn't placing a bet, the chances are you'll need to go into My Account to do it. This is the part of the Web site that helps you manage your account.

If you don't have a Betfair account yet, go to Chapter 2 on Opening a Betfair Account.

Before you can do anything in My Account, you need to log in. Here's how:

1. **Go to the Betfair homepage at `www.betfair.com`.**

   In the top right-hand part of the screen, you see a white box saying Username.

2. **Type your Username.**

3. **Click in the box to the right of Username and type your Password.**

4. **Either hit the return key or click Login.**

   Depending on the computer you are using, you may be asked if you're sure you want to continue.

5. **Click Yes.**

   You're now logged in to your Betfair account.

Should you need to leave your computer unattended for any reason, make sure that you log out of your account to prevent others using it. In the top right-hand part of the screen, click Logout, and you return to the original Betfair homepage.

After you log in, click My Account at the top of the screen. The My Account screen (shown in Figure 3-1) appears, with 13 menu options down the left-hand side of the screen. The following sections describe each option.

Figure 3-1: The My Account screen.

Account Summary

The Account Summary screen gives you a brief overview of what's going on with your account. This screen shows your account balance and current exposure. Your *current exposure* refers to any unsettled bets you may have.

The screen also shows how much money you have left to bet with or withdraw. This amount is basically your account balance minus your current exposure.

The Exposure Limit is a pre-set figure that prevents you betting more than this amount in a specified period. The default setting is £5,000, but if you reach the big time and want to bet more, you can quickly alter it by calling the Betfair Helpdesk.

Finally, the screen shows your current discount rate and the number of Betfair Points and Holidays that you have. Discount rates, points, and the like are all covered in detail in Chapter 5.

Account Statement

Account Statement shows a running progress of your account over the last month: what bets you've placed, what money you've transferred in or out, and what commission you've paid (I explain commission in Chapter 5). The Account Statement is similar to a bank statement.

You can filter what transactions are shown in the Account Statement, such as viewing only deposits and withdrawals, by choosing from the various options in the drop down menu at the top.

The Account Statement can run to several pages and the total number of pages is shown at the bottom of the page.

Deposit Funds

To deposit funds, simply enter the amount you want to deposit, your credit card's security code, and your account Password, and then click Make Deposit.

You can find your card's security code, which is the last three digits of the number on the signature strip, on the back of the card.

The deposited money should appear in your account immediately.

Withdraw Funds

This screen shows a summary of all the cards you have registered to an account.

To withdraw money, enter the amount you want to withdraw and your account Password, and then click Withdraw Funds.

Although deposits from cards are usually instant, withdrawals can take between two and five days to appear in your bank account.

My Card Details

You can manage the cards that you have registered to your account with this option. Up to three cards can be registered at any one time.

To change the details of an existing card (such as a new expiry date), click on Modify Card Details.

To add a new card, click on Add Card Details and enter the card details. You can give a nickname to each card so that you can easily remember which card it is. I talk about depositing and withdrawing money in Chapter 2.

Current Bets

This option is one of the most useful features of the site because it allows you to quickly see what bets you're currently involved with.

Use the drop down menu to select the bets you want to see – unmatched or matched (see Chapter 5 for more details on unmatched and matched bets). A full list appears, showing the market the bet is in, the selection, whether it's a back or lay bet, how much you've staked, and at what odds.

If you want to review a bet in more detail, just click the underlined market name, and you return to the market where you can review your position.

You can also use this section to quickly cancel unmatched bets. Select a bet, using the tick box on the right-hand side of each bet, and then click Submit to automatically cancel any unmatched bets. Unmatched bets are explained in detail in Chapter 5.

Betting History

You can use Betting History to view every bet that you have placed over the last three months.

Using the various drop down menus, select which type of bet to search for, the sport, and the date range, and then click Get History.

If you want to analyse a lot of bets, click the Download to Spreadsheet link to automatically save the search into a Microsoft Excel spreadsheet. You can then play around with the spreadsheet as you wish.

Betting P&L

Like Betting History, Betting P&L allows you to view your profit and loss history over a period of up to three months.

Select the time period to search by and click Get P&L. Your profit (hopefully) or loss by sport appears at the top of the page.

Click any one of the sports to see a run down of your P&L for each market you've bet on in that particular sport.

Winning on Betfair is all about being analytical. Lots of people tell you that they perform best when betting on a particular sport, but when you show them the breakdown of their betting history, it turns out that they weren't the cricket specialist they thought, but that actually snooker is where they perform best. This kind of insight can help to improve your betting.

My Profile

My Profile shows all the personal details that Betfair holds about you. If any of these details become out of date, just click Edit in the relevant section and update them.

My Security

My Security lists all the computers that have logged in to your account, on what day, and at what time.

If you ever spot a computer that you don't recognise shown here, change your password immediately and call the Betfair Helpdesk.

Betfair Points Statement

The commission you pay to Betfair (I cover commission in detail in Chapter 5) is based on the number of Betfair Points (also covered in Chapter 5) you have.

Every Betfair Point you earn is shown in this statement. Using the drop down menu at the top of the screen, you can search back to show the last three months of your Betfair Point history.

Betfair Holidays

Your Betfair Points decay at a rate of 15 per cent a week. If using the site regularly, depreciation is likely to have little effect on your Discount Rate.

But if you are going to be away for a week or more, book a Betfair Points Holiday to stop your total being reduced.

Refer And Earn

Betfair runs a scheme called Refer and Earn that can be a useful way of supplementing your betting bank. It requires that you get your friends to open an account using your unique Refer and Earn code, which you can find in this section.

This section shows who you've referred and how much money you have been paid as a result. I explain how Refer and Earn works, in Chapter 2.

Customising Your Betting

There are around 7,000 markets available every week on Betfair. This is great as it means there's plenty of choice about what to bet on.

The downside is that sometimes it can take forever to navigate to the actual event you want to bet on.

As most of us have only a few things that we're ever going to bet on, the My Markets function can really avoid a lot of wasted time.

To set up your favourite markets, follow these steps:

1. **On the left-hand side of the screen, click My Markets.**

   A screen that lists all the sports and events you can bet on appears.

2. **Choose the markets that you use most regularly.**

   For example, if you're interested in betting only on the Australian Open tennis, you can ensure that this is the only thing that appears in your menu when you log in. Simply click Tennis, Grand Slams, and then the blue arrow to the right of Australian Open.

3. Click Save at the bottom of the window.

Now, whenever you log in, the only thing that appears in your menu is the sport or event you set up, as shown in Figure 3-2.

Figure 3-2: Managing what markets you see.

Being Part of the Betfair Community

The idea of using an online chatroom is anathema to lots of us. The thought of having to read reams of drivel posted by people with nothing better to do is off-putting.

I'm not a big advocate of chatrooms. In fact, I've never used any. But I do use the Betfair Forum.

I'm not suggesting that on the Betfair Forum there isn't a fair amount of drivel, but wade through this and you can find some very helpful discussions about sports and betting.

If you've got a question, or are trying out a particular type of betting for the first time, it makes sense to ask a community of people who are doing the same thing.

You can access the Betfair Forum, shown in Figure 3-3, by clicking Forum at the top of the homepage. The Forum contains three main sections:

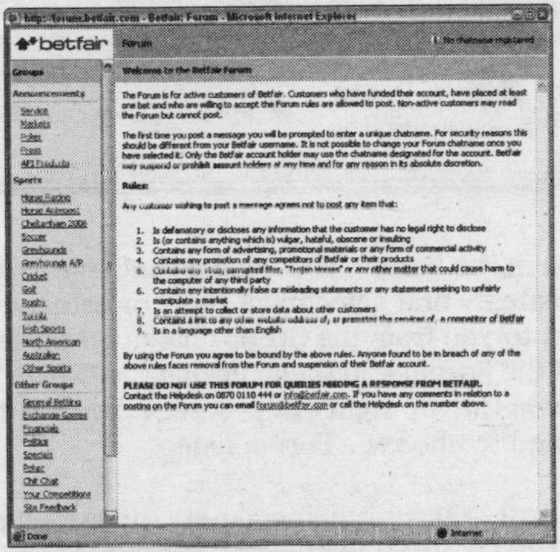

Figure 3-3: Become a forumite!

✔ **Announcements:** Used by Betfair to pass on information to all customers.

✔ **Sports:** Where you can post and read comments on a variety of sports betting.

✔ **Other groups:** Where you can post and read comments on anything you can imagine!

The Long Fellow

The Betfair Forum is a febrile place. Postings do not last long before they 'fall off the bottom'; in fact, a posting lasting longer than 24 hours is good going. But occasionally, a posting captures the imagination of forumites and enough of them respond to keep the posting alive.

In early August 2005, a Betfair customer with the chatname 'The Slug' started a posting entitled 'Piggott stories' with a request for any stories or recollections about the ex-champion jockey Lester Piggott, in the run-up to Lester's 70th birthday. Four months and over 3,000 postings later, the thread eventually fell into the dustbin of Forum history, but only after becoming one of the longest established threads in Betfair history.

To post in the Forum, you need a chatname, which you can create by first selecting a sport or category that is of interest to you from the Groups menu on the left hand side of the Forum and then clicking the Create Topic button on the top right of the screen. You will be prompted to choose a Forum name.

For security reasons, just make sure it's substantially different from your Username and Password. And you may want to think twice about using a Forum name that too closely resembles your own name– sometimes anonymity can be useful and you never know who might be reading your posting!

Chapter 4

Choosing Your Market

. . . .

In This Chapter
▶ Deciding what to bet on
▶ Getting to a market
▶ Understanding the different types of markets

. . . .

I know of one Betfair customer who makes a decent
profit from betting solely on markets that aim to predict who is going to be evicted from various reality TV
shows. During one run of Big Brother in the UK, he made
enough money to buy a small family car.

I'm not sharing this story to make you suddenly dive for
the remote control and start betting on the latest gem
from the world of reality TV shows, but to illustrate that
you have lots to choose from on Betfair. Although special-
ising is advised, it doesn't necessarily have to be in the
obvious betting markets.

In this chapter, I look at some of the different types of
events you can bet on and how you can find the markets
on the Betfair site. I also take a look at some of the different styles of markets available.

Betting: From Bandy to the BAFTAs

Betfair is all about matching up people with different opinions. But this doesn't mean that it's a free-for-all where Betfair tries to match up any request that a customer has.

Although it would be great to allow someone to come on the site and say 'I'd like to bet that my five-year-old son will win an Olympic gold medal', not many other people would be interested in laying the bet. Also, Betfair needs to make sure that the rules of any bet are clear: is there a time limit by which he needs to win the medal? Do both summer and winter Olympics count?

Providing this service for every bet that a person might want to make would require a lot of effort for no reward.

So Betfair offers markets. A *market* is a predefined event that customers can bet on.

Markets are selected based on Betfair's experience of what customers want to bet on. Betfair is always happy to try new markets on request, but these markets are closely monitored and if no one bets on them, they are unlikely to be tried again. (Not to worry, plenty of options remain.)

I haven't got the space here to detail every single item you can bet on, and quite frankly in many areas I don't have the expertise. However, in the following sections I talk about the range of things you can bet on, so that you can decide what you're most interested in.

Broadly speaking, you can bet on four different types of things: sports, financials, politics, and specials.

Betting on sports

Sports betting accounts for the majority of betting on Betfair, and you can bet on almost any sport you can think of.

Of course, all the expected sports are included, such as horse-racing, soccer, greyhound racing, cricket, American sports, tennis, and golf, plus some less likely sports, such as chess, sailing, badminton, and bandy (a sort of hockey played on ice).

Betting on financials

Financial betting has become increasingly popular in the last 20 years, and Betfair offers a wide selection of financial markets to choose from.

These markets include various stock exchange indices (London, New York, Frankfurt, and so on) as well as items such as house prices, interest rates, and oil prices.

Betting on politics

Betting on politics is becoming increasingly popular – over £19 million was matched on the 2004 US Presidential Election.

Betfair: the most accurate poll

Recent studies in the US and Australia concluded that when it comes to predicting the results of elections, Betfair offers a far more accurate indicator than regular opinion polls. In one study, the author described Betfair as a 'high-tech crystal ball'.

When you realise that opinion polls consist of a small sample of people with no reason to give accurate answers to questions, there's every reason that Betfair would be more accurate. After all, Betfair's political markets have thousands of people backing up their opinions with real money — a much more accurate indicator of voting intent.

Betfair customers' prescience was seen to good measure in both the Australian and US elections of 2004. All the opinion polls were viewing the elections as being neck-and-neck, but Betfair customers showed that the Australian Coalition and George Bush were clear favourites to win in their respective races — which they did!

Betfair offers a full range of markets for would-be politicos to bet on. These markets include who will win elections, who the next leaders of parties will be, what the result of important votes will be, and all manner of things.

Betting on specials

Special betting is a catch-all area for anything that doesn't fit in one of the other categories, such as betting on reality TV shows, award ceremonies, Miss World, and the weather.

Some of the things you can bet on still amaze me. While touring the Betfair site, I came across a market as to whether there would be a white Christmas in Finland. Doesn't it always snow in Finland in December? After all, isn't that where Father Christmas comes from?

Getting to a Betting Market

You can navigate to the market that you want in two ways: either use the menu or use the fastlinks (see Figure 4-1).

Using the menu

Everything is contained within the main menu on the left-hand side of the Betfair Homepage. To access a market, simply click the event you are interested in.

Some sports have lots of different elements to them, and you may have to click on a number of submenus before reaching the market you want to bet on.

For example, to bet on the soccer match between Bayern Munich and Mainz being a draw, you would have to click through six different menus: Soccer >German Soccer > Bundesliga >Fixtures >Bayern Munich v Mainz >Match Odds.

If you consistently navigate to the same markets, you can customise the markets that you see by using the My Markets function (see Chapter 3).

Using the fastlinks

The fastlinks in the centre and right-hand side of the homepage offer a much faster and more efficient way to get to the market you are interested in.

The team at Betfair tries to put the most popular markets in the centre of the homepage (and this list varies depending what country you are viewing the site from). So an important cricket match broadcast on TV is likely to be shown in this central area.

The right-hand side of the homepage displays a list of all events that are about to start, and all events that are in-play today.

Figure 4-1: Choose one of two ways to get to your market.

Understanding the Different Types of Market

Most markets on Betfair are straightforward – you're asked to predict what will happen in an event. For example, will a soccer team win, lose, or draw?

The best piece of advice I can give for using Betfair – advice that I repeat a number of times in this book – is always read the market rules to ensure that you understand exactly what you're betting on. You can find the market rules in every Betfair market, on the right-hand side of the screen, under the tab titled Rules. If you are ever unsure what you're betting on, don't bet!

You don't need to understand every type of Betfair market right away. Some are quite complex, and there's enough to keep you occupied to mean that you don't have to get involved in the more complicated markets if you don't want to. So if you're new to Betfair, skip the next section and come back to it when you're interested.

Although most markets are straightforward, some are a little unusual, such as place, handicap, range, and line.

Place markets

A place market allows people to bet on an event that has more than one possible winner. Most markets have only one possible result. However, some *place* markets have a number of possible results.

For example, in a golf tournament, Betfair may run a market on who will be placed in the top four competitors at the end of the tournament. This clearly has more than one possible result.

Place markets are run for all kinds of events, including snooker tournaments, soccer leagues and reality TV shows. But the most popular types of place markets are in horse-racing where, depending on the race, you can bet on a horse to finish in the top two, three or four positions and still win your bet.

You should remember two crucial things when betting in place markets:

✔ A 'place' includes first place. Very often people assume that they are betting only that something will place second or third, and they forget that first place is also counted as a 'place'.

✔ Always ensure that you check the Rules section of the market so that you know how many places are up for grabs.

Handicap markets

Handicap markets are used in a couple of instances: to make a potentially one-sided event more interesting from a betting perspective, and/or to eliminate the possibility of a draw.

Making things interesting

Rugby union often features established international sides such as Australia or France taking on less established teams. Betting on a straight result is often a non-event. Shocks do happen, but much more commonly the established team wins by a large number of points.

To make things more interesting, the established team might be given a handicap of – 20.5 by Betfair, meaning that they start with this as a virtual points deficit. This handicap means that the established team has to win by at least 21 points to 'win' the match. Handicapping in this way evens the contest up, and makes the match much more interesting to bet on.

Half-points are frequently used in handicap markets to eliminate the possibility of a draw.

Asian handicaps

An *Asian handicap* refers to a particular type of soccer betting that was initially popular in Asia, but is becoming commonplace elsewhere (see Figure 4-2).

Two main types of Asian handicap bets exist.

Figure 4-2: Betting on the Asian handicap.

In the first type, a team might be given a handicap of –1.5. This score is added to the actual match score for the purpose of the bet. If the team wins by two goals or more, they are deemed a winner in the handicap market. If not, they are deemed the loser. A draw is not possible in this instance.

In the second type of Asian handicap bet, the handicap is a whole goal (– 1.0, – 2.0, and so on). In this case, if the game is drawn when the handicap is applied, bets are declared void.

Sometimes, a team is given two handicaps, such as – 0 and – 0.5. In this example, the stake is divided between the two handicaps. So if you have £100 on a team with a – 0 and – 0.5 handicap, you are actually betting £50 on one and £50 on the other. If the team draws, the bet on the – 0 is voided and the bet on the – 0.5 handicap is lost. If the team wins, both bets are winners.

Range betting

If you want to bet on something like the total number of runs, goals, or points in a contest, range betting is for you. In range betting you're asked to 'Buy' or 'Sell' a particular value.

Your profit or loss is your stake multiplied by the difference between the level you struck your bet at and the actual total.

For example, if you buy runs in a cricket match at a level of 150 for £10, you make £10 profit for every run over that figure that is scored. Conversely, you lose that figure for every run under that amount that is scored.

Range betting always has a minimum and maximum score so that the extent of winnings or losses is always known. These are detailed in the Rules tab on the right-hand side of any market.

Line betting

Line betting also focuses on a total that is returned for a particular contest. However, line betting is an even money bet, meaning that your stake is not multiplied dependent on the final total.

For example, in a tennis match, you think that 24 aces will be served. The 'line' for the match is 28 aces. If you sell the line for £100 and less than 28 aces are served, you win £100. If more than 28 aces are served, you lose your £100 stake.

Part II
Let's Get Betting

The 5th Wave
By Rich Tennant

"Okay, I'm on the Betfair page. Let's see, Rubgy...
Tennis... Golf... here it is-Volcanoes."

In this part . . .

*N*ow, it's time to actually start betting. After all, that's why you're here.

In this part we look at betting basics and how you place your first bet. There's a quick maths lesson and we look at why *value* is the key to long-term betting profits.

We also look at in-play betting and assess some initial strategies for winning.

Chapter 5

Placing Your First Bet

* *

In This Chapter

▶ Getting a grip on betting basics

▶ Having your first back and lay bet

▶ Requesting better odds than are available

▶ Understanding how Betfair makes money

* *

An old Chinese proverb says that a long journey begins with the first step. And Betfair is no exception, except that this journey begins with your first bet.

This chapter walks you through the basics of placing a bet, backing and laying at the odds you want, and working out how much commission you pay Betfair when you win.

Understanding the Basics

A *bet* is where you risk an amount of money when predicting a future event.

A bet requires two parties – a backer who thinks something will happen, and a layer who thinks it won't.

Any bet consists of four key elements:

- ✔ **The stake** is the amount of money being risked by the backer.

- ✔ **The odds** are the rate at which the bet is to be calculated. Betfair uses decimal odds, such as 1.43, 5.2, and 60.0. Although decimal odds can take some time to get used to if you've grown up with something different, they're far simpler to understand than other systems.

- ✔ **The return** is the amount of money that is returned to the backer if his prediction is right. It includes the stake and the profit. To calculate the return from any bet, simply multiply the stake by the odds.

- ✔ **The profit/liability** is the amount of money that the backer wins if his prediction is right. To calculate the profit, simply subtract the stake from the return. This figure is also the amount of money that the layer loses.

For example, say that you back Roger Federer because you think he is going to win the US Open tennis. You stake £100 at odds of 2.12. Your prediction is right, and Federer wins the tournament. The return is £212, which is made up of £112 in profit and the original £100 stake. The person who laid you the bet has a liability of £112.

Backing and Laying

Betfair finds people with opposing views about an event and matches them together – one backer and one layer.

Backing

Backing is staking money that something will happen and making a profit if you're right.

If you think that Ivan Basso is going to win cycling's Tour de France, you may risk £100 of your money (your stake) at odds of 4.3. If you're right, and Ivan Basso goes on to win the Tour de France, you receive £430 (£100 × 4.3). This amount is made up of your original stake of £100 and your profit of £330.

Make sure that you understand the rules of any market you're betting in. (You can find them under the Rules tab on the right-hand side of any market.) For example, if you're betting on whether you'll have a white Christmas, do you know what constitutes a white Christmas? Make sure that you familiarise yourself with what you're betting on before risking any money.

Instead of spending hours going through numerous examples, the best way to get your head around backing is by placing your first back bet:

1. **Navigate to a market of your choice.**

   Check out Getting to a Betting Market in Chapter 4 if you don't know how to do so.

2. **Choose the selection you want to back – in other words, the selection you think will win the event.**

   You see a blue box to the right of the selection with two numbers in it. The top number is the best odds available to back the selection at. The bottom number is the amount of money available to back at those odds (the maximum stake you can have on). In the example of a horse-race in Figure 5-1, Misty Future is available to back at best odds of 12.5 to a maximum stake of £35.

   The figure below the odds is the amount of money available to back at those odds, but you don't have to bet that amount. You can bet as much as you like, and Betfair will do its best to match you up with someone who disagrees.

3. **Click the blue square to the right of your selection. The bet that you are requesting will appear on the right-hand side of the screen in the Place Bets tab.**

4. **Click the Your Stake box in the Place Bets tab on the right-hand side of the screen.**

5. **Enter the stake you want to place on the bet.**

   As you're just placing a practice bet, I suggest using the minimum stake of £2.

   The minimum bet on Betfair is £2. Although you can theoretically have as much money on any bet as you like, keep to the minimum until you're confident that you know what you're doing.

6. Click Submit.

Betfair displays a confirmation screen to make sure that you're happy with the bet.

7. If you agree with the bet, click Yes.

Your back bet is now placed. You see a series of green or red numbers appear under each selection in the market. These numbers show you how much you win (green) or lose (red), depending on which selection wins the event.

Figure 5-1: Placing a £2 back bet on Misty Future at odds of 12.5.

Betfair always shows you a confirmation screen after you submit your bet. You can stop its appearance by unchecking Verify Bets at the bottom of the Place Bets tab on the right-hand side of the screen.

Keeping things simple

Betfair allows you to bet in lots of ways that weren't possible before. This is great, but you might not want all the options, you might just want to be able to place a straightforward back bet.

Betfair are due to launch a simplified option in March 2006 that will allow customers to look at an Express View of the site. This option will allow customers to only back a selection, and there will be much less information on the screen.

If you want to use the simplified product, click on Express View. Otherwise, choose Full View, where there is a lot more fun to be had!

Laying

Laying is staking money that something will not happen and making a profit if you're right.

If you think that Ivan Basso hasn't got a chance of winning cycling's Tour de France, you may decide to lay him for £100 at odds of 4.3. By laying, you're essentially offering someone else the chance to back him with a stake of £100. If your opponent is right, you owe them £330 ((100 × 4.3) – 100), but if she's wrong, you keep her £100 stake.

When laying, the amount of money you enter is the backer's stake that you're prepared to accept at those odds, not the amount of money you're prepared to risk. The amount of money you're risking is the backer's stake multiplied by the odds (minus one). For example, if you lay £200 at 1.86, you're risking £172 (200 × (1.86 – 1)).

Placing a lay bet is similar to placing a back bet (see preceding section):

1. **Navigate to a market of your choice.**

   Check out Getting to a Betting Market in Chapter 4 if you don't know how to do so.

2. **Choose the selection you want to lay – in other words, the selection you think will *not* win the event.** To the right of the selection, you see a pink box with two numbers in it. The top number is the best odds available to lay the selection at. The bottom number is the amount of money available to lay at those odds. In the example of a horse-race in Figure 5-2, Presentandcorrect is available to lay at odds of 2.24 to a maximum stake of £35.

3. **Click the pink square to the right of your selection. The bet that you are requesting will appear on the right-hand side of the screen in the Place Bets tab.**

4. **Click the Backer's Stake box in the Place Bets tab on the right-hand side of the screen.**

5. **Enter the stake you want to accept on the bet.**

   As you're just placing a practice bet, I suggest using the minimum stake of £2. Figure 5-2 shows that by laying Presentandcorrect for £2 at 2.24, you're risking £2.48 (2 × (2.24 – 1)).

6. **Click Submit.**

   Betfair shows you a confirmation screen to make sure that you're happy with the bet you are placing.

7. If you're happy with the bet, click Yes.

Your lay bet is now placed. You see a series of
green or red numbers appear under each selection in the market. These numbers show you how
much you win (green) or lose (red), depending
on which selection wins the event.

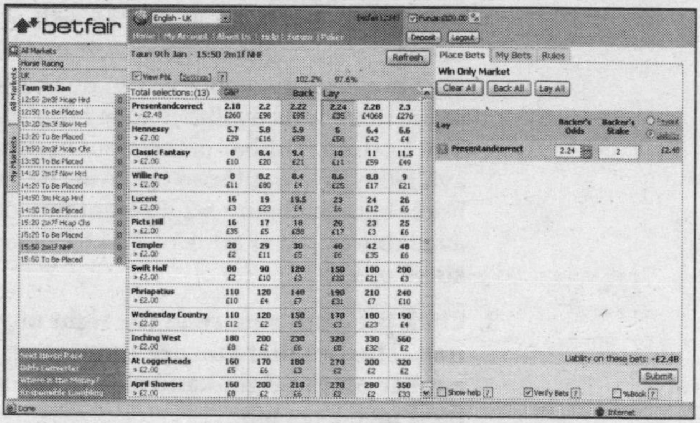

Figure 5-2: Placing a £2 lay bet on Presentandcorrect at odds of 2.24.

Asking for Better Odds

You don't always have to place straightforward bets at
odds already offered by other Betfair customers. You
have the option of asking for better odds than are currently being advertised. This option allows you to see
whether any other Betfair customers are prepared to take
you on.

Betting on the move

You can't always be in front of your computer when you want to have a bet, so a good idea is to have a backup way of accessing Betfair. For example, you may have backed a Rugby League team to win a match and hear on the radio while driving that a key player is injured and won't start the match. Without an alternative way of accessing the site, you won't be able to manage your bets on the market.

The most straightforward way of accessing Betfair on the move is by calling the Telbet service on 0870 90 80 121 (UK) or +44 208 834 8060 (International). When you call, a broker asks for your Telephone Account Number (TAN), which is located in the My Profile section of My Account. Ask the broker what market and selection you're interested in, and she advises the best currently available back and lay odds. The broker can carry out any bet you want to make on your behalf.

The major disadvantage of Telbet is that you can only use the service if you're staking at least £50.

Another option is to subscribe to a mobile Betfair application that you can access through a mobile phone or PDA. The minimum bet through mobile applications is £2. For more information about these products, go to http://bdp.betfair.com/apisolutions.php.

For example, say that you want to back Phil Taylor to win the World Darts Championship, but feel that at 1.55 the odds are too short (you want a bigger return for your money). No problem. You just ask to back Phil Taylor at 1.57 and see whether anyone takes you up on the bet.

To ask for bigger odds, complete the following steps:

1. **Navigate to a market of your choice.**

2. **Choose the selection you want to back.**

   Say that the best odds available to back the selection are 2.28, as in the example of Manchester United in a soccer match shown in Figure 5-3.

3. **Click the blue square to the right of your selection. The bet that you are requesting will appear on the right-hand side of the screen in the Place Bets tab.**

4. **Click the Backer's Stake box in the Place Bets tab on the right-hand side of the screen.**

5. **Enter the stake you want to place on the bet.**

6. **Using the arrows next to the Your Odds box, adjust the odds upwards to the odds you' want.**

   In the example shown in Figure 5-3, I ask for odds of 2.32, rather than the currently best available 2.28.

7. **Click Submit. The confirmation screen will appear.**

8. **If you're happy with the bet, click Yes.**

   Your back bet has now been placed on the system. Now you just wait to see whether anyone is prepared to match you. I explain how this works in Figuring Out Matched and Unmatched Bets, below.

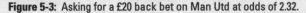

Figure 5-3: Asking for a £20 back bet on Man Utd at odds of 2.32.

You can do exactly the same when you want to lay a
selection, but in this case, you need to decrease the odds
you offer in Step 6 to decrease your liability. This is
where I always used to get confused – if you're backing
you want bigger odds to increase your potential winnings. But if you're laying you want smaller odds to
decrease your liability.

Figuring Out Matched and Unmatched Bets

Betfair matches up people with different opinions on how
an event will unfold, and a bet is struck. That's the
theory, at least!

In reality, one person is rarely matched directly against another. The more common situation is that one person is matched against many.

For example, if you want to back Pakistan to win the Cricket World Cup for £1,000 at odds of 10.5, it may be that one person matches £100 of the bet, another matches £432 of it, and a third matches the remaining £468 to give you a fully matched bet.

To view the status of your bet, click the My Bets tab on the right-hand side of the screen as seen in Figure 5-4. You see how much of your bet has been matched and how much is unmatched.

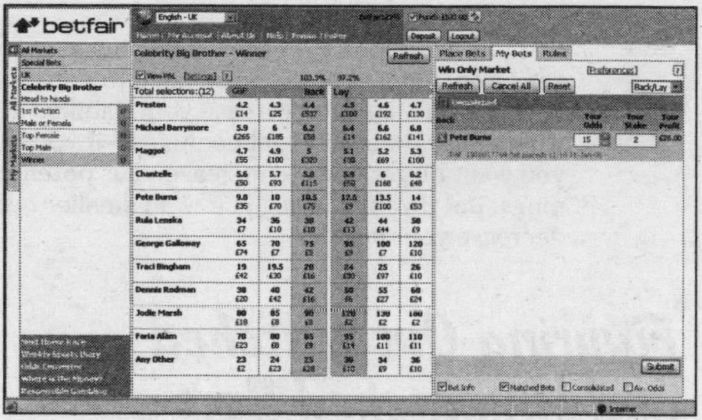

Figure 5-4: You can manage any unmatched or partially matched bets using the My Bets tab.

Betfair always does the best it can!

In December 2005, a horse called Wodhill Gold was the favourite for a race at Wolverhampton race-course, being available to back at odds of around 4.0. During the contest, Wodhill Gold began to struggle.

Four Betfair customers, however, retained their faith in the horse and asked to back it in-running at various odds up to 55.0 – much bigger than the odds available before the start of the race.

In a strange turn of events, during the few seconds that elapsed while the customers were entering their bet requests, the horse began to struggle further, and another Betfair customer offered to lay the horse at the maximum odds of 1,000.

Because Betfair uses a queuing system that always matches up customers at the best possible odds, those who had wanted to back the horse at odds of 55.0 and lower suddenly found themselves matched at 1,000!

This kind of thing happens everyday on Betfair, although this instance is unusual because Wodhill Gold, who looked to have no chance of winning at halfway, recovered dramatically to snatch victory on the line.

Good news for the Betfair customers, who won nearly £100,000 from these small speculative bets. Less good news for the one customer who laid the bets!

If some or all your bet is unmatched, you can cancel it or adjust either the stake or the odds and then resubmit the bet.

Whenever resubmitting a bet, be aware that the new part of any bet goes automatically to the back of the queue. So if you're increasing your stake, the original bet stays where it is, but a separate bet that increases the total staked to the desired amount is now at the back of the queue at those odds

Paying Commission

You may think that Betfair is some benevolent enterprise that offers a free marketplace for customers to bet against each other and doesn't expect anything in return. Unfortunately, this generosity is not the case!

Betfair makes money by charging you a commission on your net winning in a market.

If you lose money in a market, you pay no commission.

Every market on Betfair has a Market Base Rate (MBR) that is the starting point for calculating any commission that you pay. The MBR is set at 5 per cent for most markets. The MBR can be found in the Rules tab on the right-hand side of any market.

All customers also have a Discount Rate (DR) that is determined by their number of Betfair Points (BPs). The more you use Betfair, the more BPs you earn, and the greater your DR becomes.

To work out the commission you pay in a market you first have to reduce the MBR by your DR. For example, if the MBR is 5 per cent and your DR is 40 per cent then the percentage of your winnings you pay to Betfair as commission is 3 per cent (5 – (5 × 0.4)). Now multiply this number by your net winnings. If you won £20, say, you would pay £0.60 (20 × 0.03).

Chapter 6

Doing the Maths

● ●

In This Chapter

▶ Identifying value

▶ Understanding what the odds actually mean

▶ Assessing which bets represent good value

▶ Betting more than once on an event

● ●

1 don't remember the first time I had a bet. My dad was a horse-racing fan and he took me to the races a lot as a kid. On one of those occasions, I must have placed my first bet (with his help). The fact that I can't remember probably tells you something about how young I was, how unconcerned my dad was about breaking the law, and why I now work for a betting company!

Whenever that first bet happened, at some point I became hooked – probably because I liked the sensation of winning money for nothing.

But when you're trying to make long-term profit from betting, this motivation is just about the worst kind. Long-term profits are not achieved by finding winners, but by finding value.

In this chapter, I explain the concept of value, look at how a market is actually constructed, and what the odds really mean. I outline some different ways of assessing value bets, and describe why having more than one bet on an event can sometimes be worthwhile.

Being Value Conscious

After having a losing bet, professional punters often seem fairly unperturbed; they may utter something along the lines of, 'it was the right bet to have.'

But how can this be the case? The bet lost! Maybe professional punters are unwilling to accept that they are ever wrong (and a fair few of them are!), or maybe something else is going on.

Professional gamblers know that winning every time is not the most important thing. The important thing is that when you do win, the profit makes up for any previous losses and then some.

Value is defined as getting better odds on the event you are betting on than the chance of it occurring.

The best example of value is tossing a coin. If you toss a coin and call 'heads' a thousand times, you'll be right roughly half the time.

But is 'heads' a good bet in every instance? The answer is, of course, that it depends on the odds. If someone offers you 2.5 (meaning that you win one and a half times your stake every time heads comes up), you win in the long run. If someone offers you 1.5 (meaning you win half your stake every time heads comes up), you lose in the long run. The true odds of it being heads are 2.0.

The key to winning on Betfair is having an appreciation of whether you're getting better odds than the actual chance of something happening.

Adding It All Up

Determining whether something has value requires an understanding of the maths behind betting.

If maths isn't your thing (and one or two of my retired maths teachers will certainly tell you that it was never mine), please don't put the book down just yet. The maths is fairly straightforward, and necessary if you're going to be a winner on Betfair.

Every betting market on Betfair, for every event, has a series of odds available for people to back. Traditional bookmakers call this set of odds their 'book' (hence the name 'bookmaker').

Making a book is how traditional bookmakers ensure that they make long-term profits.

Table 6-1 shows a typical book on a Rugby Union international.

Table 6-1	A Book on a Rugby Match	
Team	**Odds**	**Implied Percentage Chance**
New Zealand	1.5	66.6%
France	3.0	33.3%
Draw	10.0	10%
100%		110%

New Zealand is the favourite to win the match and is being offered at odds of 1.5. These odds imply that New Zealand has a 66.6 per cent chance of winning the match, or put another way, that the team is expected to win twice out of every three times the game is played.

To work out the implied percentage chance that any odds represent, simply do the following calculation: 100/ odds.

France is offered at 3.0, implying that the team has a 33.3 per cent (100/3) chance of winning. The draw is offered at 10.0, implying that the result will be a draw 10 per cent (100/10) of the time.

The crucial point is that the implied percentages calculated from the odds add up to 110 per cent and yet the real chance of any of the three outcomes occurring is 100 per cent – one of these outcomes must happen. Bookmakers build in the extra 10 per cent into the odds offered to ensure that they make a profit in the long run.

The 110 per cent figure is known as an *overround*. If the figure ever drops below 100 per cent, the book goes *overbroke,* because the possibility then exists of you backing all the selections to the correct stake and guaranteeing yourself a profit.

The 110 per cent figure doesn't mean that a bookmaker always makes a profit on every market he offers. If a disproportionate amount of money is bet on one selection that goes on to win, the bookmaker loses money. But he knows that as long as the overround is big enough, in the long run he'll l always make money.

Betfair displays the overround above the back and lay columns of every market. The lower the overround, the more competitive the market.

Getting the Value

If value is getting better odds than the actual chance of something happening, all you need to assess is the chance of something happening so that you know the right bet to make. Getting value is that simple!

A number of ways exist in which you can do this, but all the approaches fit broadly into two areas: using your knowledge of the sport or using data.

Using your knowledge

Using your know how to define the percentage chance of something happening is not an exact science, but if you're methodical in how you think it through, you can identify value bets.

For example, you're watching a cricket test match between Pakistan and England from Bangalore. In the first innings, England has scored 153 – 6, and so Pakistan is now favourite to win the match, being available to back at 1.65, with the draw at 2.7 and England at 20.

You have to ask yourself whether these are the right odds or not. According to the odds, Pakistan has about a 60 per cent (100/1.65) chance of winning the match, and the draw is about a 37 per cent chance (100/2.7). So at this point you have to assess the situation:

✔ Pakistan has taken a number of quick wickets, but a lot of these wickets seem to be a result of the unpredictable way that the pitch is playing. England has every chance of being able to take wickets just as quickly when Pakistan starts batting.

✔ Pakistan is 1 – 0 up in the test series, with this being the last match. As Pakistan needs only a draw to win the series, the team is unlikely to take any risks by playing for a win.

✔ So far in the series, both sides have played exceptionally slowly and the umpires have been quick to halt play because of bad light. Also, the high temperature is causing the teams to request and take a number of drinks' breaks. The reduced playing time means that a struggling side is more likely to force a draw.

On the other hand, England has not been bowling well and rumours are circulating that the team doesn't really want to be there, and that the players are looking to end the match as quickly as possible.

On the basis of all this information, you decide that Pakistan is currently being offered at too short odds; you decide to lay them at 1.65.

This approach is not especially scientific, but you have methodically assessed the situation and come to a considered opinion. You may not be right, but if your knowledge is good enough you have every reason to believe that this approach is going to reap benefits in the long run.

And this approach is applicable to all events – from TV reality shows to tennis matches.

If something seems too good to be true, it usually is. If you are analysing a market and feel that the odds are completely wrong on a particular selection, you need to ask yourself if you have all the available information to hand. Are you unaware of something that is affecting the odds?

Using data

If you have a particular aptitude for data and statistics, you can apply this knowledge to seeking value bets.

One of the most common ways that bettors do this is through the use of ratings systems.

A *ratings system* is where you try to apply a numerical value to a sporting performance. By doing this, you are better able to predict future performances.

One of the simplest ratings systems is a *league table,* where teams or individuals are given varying amounts of points depending on whether they win, lose, or draw.

For example, in soccer, when a team at the top of a league plays a team at the bottom of a league, the former is the most likely to win.

However, this example is very simplistic, and so many bettors decide to build much more complex ratings systems that include variables such as overall performance, goals scored, and goals conceded.

Many bettors also utilise trends and statistics. For example, you may know that ten out of the last ten winners of a particular horse-race had all won over a distance of at least three miles before going on to win the race in question. This trend may be invaluable in allowing you to reduce the number of 'possible' winners and decide which horses represent value.

You may also know that 80 per cent of players winning the first set of a tennis match on a particular surface, go on to win the match. Again, having this knowledge is invaluable is assessing whether an in-play bet in a tennis match represents value.

Combining knowledge and data

The reality is that very few bettors use only knowledge or data (see Using your knowledge and Using data, above). Even the most hardened data junkies usually sense-check the figures using their knowledge of a particular event.

The Hole-In-One-Gang

Disraeli's assertion of there being lies, damn lies, and statistics may be good advice when listening to the claims of a politician, but the right statistic can prove invaluable if you're a punter.

Two bettors, who later became known as the Hole-In-One-Gang, found a statistic that surprised them – in roughly one out of every two professional golf tournaments, a player achieved a hole-in-one.

However, when they asked friends and acquaintances how often they thought this event occurred, the answer was always, 'once in a blue moon!'

The pair decided to tour the country asking small independent bookmakers to quote them odds on there being a hole-in-one in any of that year's four golfing majors. Most of the bookmakers offered them huge odds, so the two bettors placed a number of relatively small bets.

That year, players scored hole-in-ones in three of the four majors, and the two men picked up just short of £1 million in winnings. Evidence, if needed, that statistics can be an invaluable tool in any betting armoury.

And taking this dual approach is the most likely way to guarantee long-term profits. Analysis of data is usually a great starting point, offering an instant view of what the correct odds should be. However, using the data alone is unlikely to be as successful as thinking through what the data is telling you.

For example, your data may tell you that a golfer has a 25 per cent chance of winning a tournament. You see that he is available at 20.0 and can't believe your luck. However, on closer inspection you notice that the tournament is played on a links course and this player has never won a links course tournament.

Combining the approaches in this way can be critical to making goods bets and eliminating bad ones.

Having More Than One Bet in a Market

Placing more than one bet on the same event is unthinkable to many people. You either think something will happen or you don't.

But if you're interested in value rather than always picking a winner, placing more than one bet on the same event may often be the right thing to do.

For example, say that you're analysing a Formula One Grand Prix. A particular team has been winning the most races of late, but you feel that today's track is particularly unsuitable to this team's car. Another team has a car that you think is going to suit the track better, and you think that each of this team's drivers has about a 10 per cent chance of winning (odds of 10.0). And yet these drivers are available at odds of 40.0 and 65.0 respectively. In this example, you may decide to back both of the drivers with a stake of £10 each as they both represent value. If the first driver wins, you win £380, if the second driver wins, you win £630. If neither driver wins, you lose your two stakes of £20.

Having more than one bet in a market in this way is known as *dutching*.

Chapter 7

Betting In-Play

• •

In This Chapter

▶ Getting a grip on in-play betting

▶ Understanding how in-play markets are managed

▶ Taking a look at some unusual in-play situations

▶ Ensuring your information source is up to the job

▶ Looking at some strategies for in-play profit

• •

*H*ow many times have you been sure that an event is going to turn out a certain way, and then changed your mind when the event started?

Maybe you think that a dart player is going to annihilate an opponent, and then realise after the first couple of games that he's struggling to hit his doubles.

Or maybe you think that a tennis player can win a match but are worried that her serve will let her down. After a few games, you realise that she's serving like a demon and wish you'd backed her to win.

Betfair gives you the opportunity to bet on many events after they've started, right up until the moment they finish – and sometimes even after they've finished!

Watching a Contest Unfold on Your PC

In-play betting is betting on an event once it has started.

That's it!

You can back and lay in exactly the same way as before an event starts. (See Chapter 5 for more on backing and laying.) The main difference is that the available odds move much more quickly as Betfair customers react to what is happening in the event.

One fascinating aspect of in-play betting is that often the Betfair market can provide as much information about an event as watching the event itself.

In fact, many Betfair customers talk about 'watching a game', when they have just been watching the odds on Betfair move back and forth.

Knowing What Is In-Play

If you plan to specialise in betting during events, you need to know which ones will go in-play.

Betfair uses a large tick, which appears on screen with a green background, shown in Figure 7-1, to indicate whether an event is in-play or not. Watch for this tick in the event menu, on the homepage, or within a market itself so you know when the event in question has started.

Figure 7-1: The famous tick tells you an event has started.

You can check which events will go in-play in three main ways:

- ✔ **By checking the In-play Today section on the Betfair Homepage.** Located on the right-hand side of the homepage, this section displays any upcoming events that you can bet on in-play.

- ✔ **By looking at the Rules tab in any market.** On the right-hand side of any market, you can see a panel. Under the Rules tab is an explanation of whether the

event in question will go in-play and, more importantly, how it will be managed (see the Managing In-
Play Markets section later in this chapter).

✔ **By checking out Betfair's TV schedule at www.bet
fair.tv.** The Betfair TV schedule outlines all the
popular events coming up that week, shows you
where you can watch them, and displays the green
tick if Betfair is going to cover the event in-play.

Not all events go in-play, so don't assume that they will –
always check the Rules tab within a market to confirm.

Managing In-Play Markets

Although you can back and lay in exactly the same way
when betting in-play, a few things are different. (See
Chapter 5 for more on backing and laying.)

In the shadow of the post

In June 2005, Rising Shadow lined
up as a well-supported favourite
for the 4 p.m. race from Newcastle:
the horse was backed at around
4.5 to win.

But by mid-race, he was struggling
at the back of the field and seemed
to have lost all chance of winning.
At that point, £41 was matched on
Rising Shadow winning at 1,000.

Two other horses, Pieter Brueghel
and Ellens Academy, were both
backed at short odds to win
the race (1.10 and 1.25 respectively), but Rising Shadow suddenly improved towards the end
of the race and flew home to
reward the big-odds backers (and
punish the big-odds layers!)

First, whenever a market goes in-play, the pre-event market is suspended, all bets waiting to be matched are cancelled, and the market is reopened.

Second, Betfair employees actively manage some in-play markets. For example, in soccer matches that are covered in-play, the market is suspended and all unmatched bets cancelled following a sending off, a penalty, or a goal. However, other markets are not actively managed.

Third, bets placed in-play are often subject to a delay. This delay varies by event and is usually between 1 and 5 seconds and is outlined in the rules section of a market. If a betting delay is in operation, a clock-face begins to rotate in the betting panel after you submit your bet. Betting delays are used to protect customers who are offering odds and then notice that something has happened that means they no longer want to offer that bet. The delay allows the customers to cancel their bets before they are matched.

Always check the rules in any market to find out whether the event is to be actively managed in-play.

Going In-Play Crazy

Betting in-play can be extraordinarily volatile, because the events that people are betting on are themselves volatile. Everyone remembers some sporting moment where a huge upset was caused, or a seemingly impossible comeback was achieved.

Just as these moments provide great sporting drama, they also provide great in-play betting drama on Betfair.

I list a number of examples in Chapter 15, but here are a few categories where things can go a bit mad.

Photo finishes and stewards' enquiries

Betfair offers in-play betting in most horse-racing markets. A market is suspended at the start of the race with all unmatched bets cancelled, and then reopened for people to bet during the race.

Even at this stage, the market can be volatile – with horses falling when looking like certain winners, or coming from nowhere to win.

The market is suspended again when the first horse passes the post. However, if a finish is particularly close and a photo is called for, or if the stewards call an enquiry (meaning the result may get changed), the market is reopened once again and customers are allowed to continue betting – something that thousands of people do!

Betting on photo finishes and stewards' enquiries is a very specialist area, so only bet on them if you feel you have a thorough understanding of what is happening.

1.01 and 1,000 betting

Certain winners nearly always trade at 1.01, the minimum odds on Betfair (meaning that a backer makes £1 profit for every £100 staked). However, the meaning of 'certain' can sometimes vary hugely! For example, in February 2003 Jimmy White and Peter Ebdon faced each other in a snooker match, and people were amazed when both players traded at 1.01!

Selections frequently trade at odds of 1.01 and yet still get beaten. It may be a soccer team that is a goal up with seconds to play, a snooker player with what looks like a match winning position, or a golfer who needs only a double bogey to win a tournament. Surprises can also happen with 'certain' losers who trade at 1,000.

Knowing Your Source of Information

Live is not always live. If you bet in-play, pin up this phrase on your computer screen.

Out! Hang on!

In May 2005, the third round of the Rome Masters witnessed an amazing tennis match, and associated Betfair market.

Andy Roddick was 7-6, 5-4 and 40-0 up in his best-of-three set match against Fernando Verdasco. Roddick served to win the match and his opponent's return was called 'out'.

For a moment, it appeared that the match was over. Roddick was backed at the minimum odds of 1.01 and Verdasco was matched at 270. But then the 'out' call was disputed. In a display of sportsmanship, Roddick conceded that it was a bad call and gave Verdasco the point.

Verdasco went on to save two more match points in the game and eventually won the match. One Betfair customer won £1,500 by backing Verdasco, for a £7 stake!

When betting on any event, you have to understand how up to date the pictures are that you're watching.

You don't need to be an expert in how pictures get to your TV screens, but you do need to be aware of one crucial fact: sometimes the pictures you're watching have been delayed.

In the UK, a number of different terrestrial and satellite channels broadcast horse-racing. All of these channels claim to show 'live' racing, but sometimes there can be more than five seconds difference between what is actually happening and the pictures being shown.

The disadvantages are obvious of betting in-play based on pictures that are delayed this much. For example, you can conceivably try to back a horse that has already fallen.

However, delayed pictures don't completely preclude you from betting in-play – as long as you're aware of the situation. I frequently bet in-play using TV pictures that I know are a few seconds delayed, but I never bet in the final stages of a race, where those few seconds can be crucial to what may have happened.

Of course, horse-racing is not the only event where you need to be aware of these issues. If you're watching a golf tournament from Korea and betting on it, the chances are that the pictures have bounced off one or more satellites before reaching your TV. Again, this fact doesn't preclude betting, but you need to be aware that someone somewhere may have access to information a second or two before you.

What's the score?

Bradley Dredge went out for the third round of the 2003 Madeira Island Open Golf Tournament with a share of the lead. At the opening hole, he shot a birdie three and all was well with his game.

Regrettably, a mistake was made on the European Tour's Web site and rather than posting '3' as his first hole score, a '30' was posted. Thinking that Dredge had lost all chance of winning the tournament, many Betfair customers began to lay the golfer on the basis of this information – out to odds of 500.

Unfortunately for the layers, Dredge went on to equal the European Tour round record by shooting 60 for an unassailable eight-stroke lead. One Betfair customer lost over £10,000, and many others lost significant sums.

This incident illustrates the importance of having full confidence in the information source you are using. And if something looks too good to be true, it probably is.

The importance of knowing how up to date your source of information may be is not solely limited to TV pictures. Radio stations broadcasting over the Internet and Web sites providing information on scores, results, and the like are all prone to being out of date and inaccurate.

Profiting from Being Nearly Right

Ten types of people exist in the world – those who understand binary, and those who don't.

This is a pretty terrible joke, but it leads me nicely to an important point: betting used to be a binary enterprise – you made a prediction before an event, and then sat back to see whether you were right or not. You weren't able to wait until a few minutes into the event to see how things were going, or change your mind mid-way through.

The ability to wait opens up a number of strategies for profit that weren't previously available. In the following sections, I outline a couple of examples, but hundreds more like these exist, and they will become apparent as you investigate in-play opportunities in your chosen event.

Know your event

The most obvious way of profiting from in-play betting is to use your knowledge of a particular event.

Many imponderables exist before an event starts, and so you have to bear in mind the difficulty of coming to a view on what will happen.

A horse has a chance as long as it gets a good start; a golfer has a chance provided he doesn't fade his drive; a cricket team has a chance as long as the pitch isn't play-ing too unpredictably.

By waiting for a few minutes into an event, you're often able to better assess some of these imponderables, and therefore bet with a lot more confidence.

Take advantage of overreaction

Betfair customers often overreact to incidents in an event, and by spotting these overreactions you can often find yourself with a value bet (for an explanation of value see Chapter 6).

A good example is the sending off of a player in a soccer match. People often assume that the numerically superior team is going to dominate the stricken team, and so the odds available on both teams alter significantly.

Frequently, however, the reduced team is able to alter their style of play and close the game down, and so people who overreacted and backed the numerically superior team at short odds often lose.

You can do your homework on these instances and get historical statistics to back up your betting decisions in-play. For example, look at a sample of soccer games when players have been sent off. What is the relationship between a player getting sent off and the number of goals the opposition goes on to score?

This kind of information often enables you to profit from the overreactions of others.

Part III
Getting Serious

The 5th Wave
By Rich Tennant

"I play a bit of Exchange Blackjack on Betfair, but I'm a pretty conservative punter. I suspect you prefer the more exotic bets."

In this part . . .

*H*ere we look at some more advanced strategies for winning on Betfair, including *trading* and *arbing*, and how your betting can be automated.

We look at what it takes to make betting your living (or at least a good second living), and on the flip side, how to recognize and deal with a betting problem.

Chapter 8

Low-Risk Betting: Trading

In This Chapter

▶ Betting with minimal risk

▶ Trading to guarantee a profit

I was at a party with a professional gambler friend of mine, and we were talking to a woman. The conversation was going badly and got worse when she found out the occupation of my friend. Looking him up and down with a disbelieving look, she exclaimed, 'You don't look like much of a risk-taker!'

For many people, the popular image of a professional gambler is of someone driving a Rolls Royce, wearing jewellery, smoking a cigar, and waving large amounts of cash around – a larger-than-life character, living on the edge, and taking innumerable risks.

And yet the popular image is completely wrong. The very point of professional gambling is to emphasise any advantage you have while minimising risk.

So, although many Betfair customers are continuing to gamble as they always have, for some, the thought of watching a race or a football match without knowing that they have already made a profit is anathema.

Buying-Low, Selling-High

In *Trading*, you back a selection at a high odds and then lay it at lower odds (or conversely, lay a selection at low odds and back it at higher odds), and in the process guarantee yourself what is called a risk-free position. I think of this method as the buy-low, sell-high of betting.

Backing is betting that something will happen. *Laying* is betting that something won't happen. (See Chapter 5 for a full explanation.)

Putting theory into practice

Golf is a good sport to illustrate how trading works in practice.

The British Open is being held at St. Andrews – a course that favours players who hit the ball a long way. Few players hit the ball harder and farther than Tiger Woods, so you back Tiger before the tournament starts for £100 at 5.0. This bet means that if Tiger lifts the title, you make a profit of £400 ((£100 × 5.0) – £100).

As you expected, Tiger outdrives his competitors on every hole, and he is three shots ahead of the field by the end of the second day. The odds on Betfair have now shortened and Tiger is available at 2.0.

At this point, you have two options: do nothing and cheer Tiger all the way home, or lay Tiger at the shorter odds to guarantee a profit, no matter what happens.

The weather forecast at St Andrews doesn't look good for the last two days of the tournament. Because you don't fancy Tiger to cope with the changing conditions, you lay him at the end of the second day for £250 at 2.0. This bet means that if Tiger lifts the title, you lose £250 to another Betfair customer ((£250 × 2.0) – £250).

But here's the clever bit! Because you've already backed Tiger at higher odds than you've just laid, you don't care what happens – you win if he wins, and you win if he loses (see Table 8-1 below).

If Tiger wins, you win £400 from your first bet. You lose £250 from your second bet. That's a net profit of £150.

If Tiger loses, you lose the £100 staked in your first bet. You win the £250 staked in your second bet. That's a net profit of £150.

This situation is sometimes referred to as a 'risk-free position', 'locking-in a profit', or an 'all-green book'. The latter term refers to the fact that having completed the trade, you have a positive, green number next to each selection in the market.

Table 8-1	Winning No Matter What		
Result of British Open	*1st bet. £100 backed at 5.0*	*2nd bet. £250 laid at 2.0*	*Net Profit (Loss)*
Tiger wins	You win £400	You lose £250	**£150**
Tiger loses	You lose £100	You win £250	**£150**

Making life easier

Working out how to create risk-free positions isn't always straightforward – especially if you have lots of bets in a market or are trying to do things quickly. So if, like me, you're not some devilish mathematical genius, adjust the Market View Settings and let Betfair do the hard work:

1. **Navigate to the market you want to bet on.**

2. **Click Settings near the top of the screen. The Market View Settings screen will appear as seen in Figure 8-1.**

3. **Check the box next to Show A Separate Future Position.**

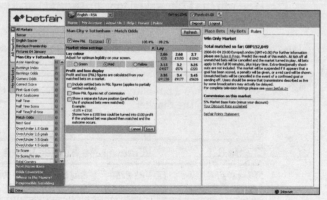

Figure 8-1: Adjusting the Market View settings.

The Market View settings allow you to assess quickly the outcome of you placing the bet you've entered.

For example, the screen may indicate – £20.00>>£4.00, meaning, 'At the moment, if this selection wins, you lose £20. If you complete the planned bet and the selection wins, you win £4'.

You can use this function to vary the odds or stake of your proposed bet, and therefore create the position that you want.

Knowing when to lock-in

No hard rules exist as to when you should try to lock-in a profit and when you should just let your original bet ride. The decision depends on your betting strategy.

If you back Tiger Woods in the British Open at odds of 6.0 and he plays well in the opening rounds, his odds will shorten. At what stage, if any, should you lay Tiger to guarantee a profit?

The concept of value is central to knowing when to lock-in. (See Chapter 6 for a full explanation of value.) If Tiger is now available at odds of 2.0, you have to ask if he has got a 50 per cent chance of winning the tournament? If you think he has a greater chance than this, in theory you are not getting value by laying him at these odds. If however, you think he has less than a 50 per cent chance of winning the tournament, you are getting value.

Unfortunately, you cannot be sure of Tiger's chances of winning the tournament at any given point. But at the very least, you should ask yourself these questions:

> ✔ What chance does the selection have of winning the event?
>
> ✔ Are the odds on offer (whether backing or laying) better than that percentage chance?
>
> ✔ Are you prepared to live by your decision if it doesn't go your way?

I know winners who always trade out of a position when they can guarantee a profit and others who would never trade out. But all these people have in common a strong opinion of whether the odds are in their favour or not.

Talk with any gambler in the world and I bet that person has a story about being unjustly denied a winning bet – a horse falling at the last fence when leading, a football team losing to a last minute goal, or Tiger Woods losing in the Open due to a change in weather conditions. The choice of whether to trade out really depends on your style of trading and attitude to risk. But the option allows you the ability to profit from being *nearly* right, even when the gods conspire to take things away from you.

Following the Market

The trading described in the section 'Buying-Low, Selling-High' still has a high level of risk. If your opinion is wrong, the opportunity to trade out may well have passed. If you could always predict the exact course of events in sport, trading would be very easy, but of course you can't. Although trading opportunities do present themselves when events move in your favour, they just as frequently do not present themselves!

No kind of trading is completely risk-free. If the market moves other than you predict, you lose money. The value of your investments can go down as well as up!

Live is not always live

One afternoon in 1985, I came home to find my dad watching the tennis from Wimbledon on TV. I told him that I thought Henri Leconte was playing well and would probably beat Boris Becker. 'I bet you he won't' was my dad's succinct reply. Within a few seconds, I had wagered my week's pocket money that my dad was wrong and sat back to watch the action. I didn't realise that I'd been had until the TV presenter spoke over the commentary to inform viewers that the BBC would continue to show replays until the rain abated. An expensive lesson, but then all the valuable ones are.

Although not as extreme, here's a similar situation to bear in mind. This year I was watching the Australian Open and noticed that odds kept disappearing as I went to bet them. Obviously, someone in Australia was enjoying a few seconds advantage over me due to the time it took the satellite pictures to cross half the world and reach my TV. So when betting on an event that has started, make sure that you have the best sources of data possible and that someone isn't enjoying an unfair advantage over you.

A different type of trader

One type of trader doesn't rely on how an event pans out, but instead makes assessments as to how the market will move prior to an event, in order to achieve the type of risk-free position described in the section above 'Buying-Low, Selling-High'. These people are closer to being financial market traders than gamblers. They are not interested in the result, or even how the event might progress: their sole concern is how the market will move prior to an event starting.

To make this assessment, these people rely on Betfair being a free market, or what economists refer to as a perfectly competitive market, where the odds available to back and lay (or buy and sell) are set by thousands of individuals competing against each other.

Supply and demand

In a perfectly competitive market, prices are set on the basis of supply and demand. If more people want to back a particular selection (because they think it will win) than want to lay it, the odds on that selection get smaller, or *shorten*. On the flip side, if more people want to lay a selection (because they think it will lose) than want to back it, the odds on that selection get bigger, or *drift*.

The analogy of the stock market is again useful to illustrate this situation. Say that a stock is trading at £1.00, and then a famous analyst suggests that the stock is a good buy in his weekly newspaper column. Lots of people take his advice and start buying the stock. Therefore, demand goes up. But unless supply also increases, the price on this stock rapidly increases above £1.00, making it harder, or less lucrative, for those who want to buy the stock.

The same happens in a Betfair market. Lots of people want to back a horse and the odds shorten, making it less lucrative for those who want to continue backing the horse.

You can see this scenario day in and day out, on every market that is traded on Betfair. I think of it as a big game of tug of war: backers on one side, layers on the other. When the amount of money on each side is equal, the odds remains constant, but as soon as an imbalance occurs (as on Auction Room in Figure 8-2) in the amount of money on either side, the odds move.

The amount of money available to back or lay on any selection appears under the odds of that selection.

Figure 8-2: Money queuing up on the lay side of the market.

A horse-racing example

In a horse-racing market, say that a lot of money is queuing-up on Auction Room on the lay side of the market (the right-hand side). This means that a lot of people want to back the horse. Conversely, on the back side of the market (the left-hand side), you don't see a large amount of money in comparison, which means that not many people want to lay the horse. Thinking about supply and demand, this scenario means that the odds are likely to shorten. (For more on this topic, see the section about supply and demand, earlier in this chapter.)

A minute later, the same market looks like Figure 8-3.

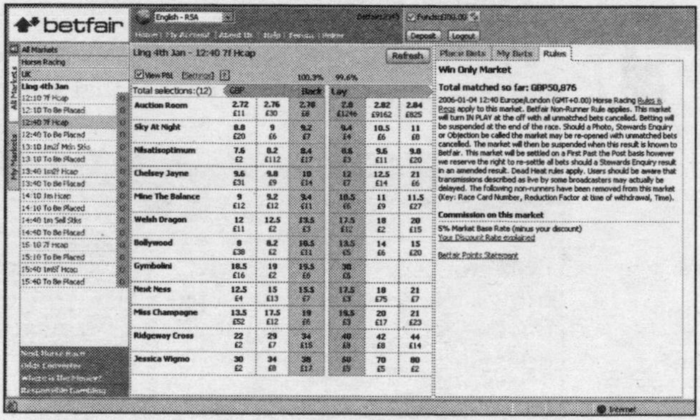

Figure 8-3: More money on the lay side of the market shorten the odds further.

The odds on Auction Room have shortened from 2.9 (Figure 8-2), down to 2.78. And the money still queuing up on the lay side of the market (see Figure 8-4), suggests that the odds are about to shorten even further.

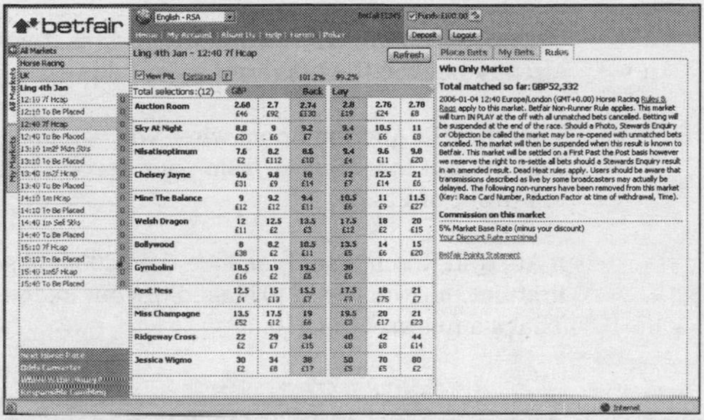

Figure 8-4: The money for Auction Room has now dried-up.

Looking at the same market just before the race goes off, the odds on Auction Room have shortened to 2.72, from the original price of 2.9.

Profiting from these market movements follows the same principles of trading described earlier in the section Buying-Low Selling-High – the only difference is that the odds increments are now smaller.

You notice that money is building up on the lay side of the market for Auction Room. You back the horse for £200 at 2.9, meaning that if Auction Room wins the race, you win £380 ((£200 × 2.9) – £200).

As you expected, the odds on Auction Room begin to shorten. A couple of minutes later, you lay Auction Room for £210 at 2.74, meaning that if Auction Room wins the race, you lose £365.40 to another Betfair customer ((£210 × 2.74) – £210).

But you don't mind if Auction Room wins, because you've already backed the horse at bigger odds.

Therefore, if Auction Room wins, you win £380 from your first bet but lose £365.40 from your second bet. That's a net profit of £14.60.

If Auction Room loses, you lose the £200 staked in your first bet but win the £210 staked in your second bet. That's a net profit of £10.

Table 8-2	Backing and laying the same selection at different odds can guarantee you a profit no matter who wins		
Result of Race	**1st bet. £200 backed at 2.9**	**2nd bet. £210 laid at 2.74**	**Net Profit (Loss)**
Auction Room wins	You win £380	You lose £365.40	**£14.60**
Auction Room loses	You lose £200	You win £210	**£10**

This example covers a horse whose odds shorten, but money can just as easily build up on the back side of a selection, causing the odds to drift.

The professional's philosophy

Some people may think that this process is a lot of effort for a tenner. In some respects this is true, but the philosophy of a professional Betfair market trader is to make low-risk trades like this frequently and often. And by taking this approach, profits can quickly add up.

Imagine completing a risk-free trade three times in a market worth £10 each time. That's £30 profit in a race. Doing that 20 times in a day equates to £600 – tax-free! Not a bad living for a few hours of work a day.

Theoretically, you can trade any market in this fashion. However, the more volatile markets are best, because they provide the opportunity for lots of odds movements – which of course are essential when you're trading. For this reason, horse-racing is a particularly popular trading sport. Lots of markets exist each day, and every one has a high level of volatility in the last ten minutes before the race is run.

Effective trading relies on your ability to make speedy bets to get that all-green book. If you're using Betfair on an old, slow computer with a dial-up Internet connection, you're probably going to miss out on a lot of bets through lack of speed. Although not essential for all types of betting on Betfair, trading really requires a decent machine and a broadband Internet connection or equivalent.

Traders sometimes use a technique called spoofing to trick others into altering the odds of a particular runner or team. Spoofing involves submitting a large bet to either back or lay a selection. When the money is seen on screen, Betfair customers tend to react to it by moving the odds in the opposite direction. You can usually tell when someone is trying to spoof a market because an amount of money will appear that is completely out of kilter with the sums seen elsewhere in the market.

Exploring More Market Strategies

The core market dynamic that moves odds in a particular direction is the amount of money available on the back and lay sides of the market. However, traders sometimes use a number of other concepts to help them assess what is likely to happen to any odds.

These concepts are again borrowed from the world of the stock market and something called technical analysis.

Technical analysis is about looking for peaks, bottoms, trends, patterns, and other factors affecting a stock's price. Technical analysts talk about a lot of largely incomprehensible things. Candlesticks. Bollinger Bands. Relative Strength Indexes. And if you want to comprehend them, I recommend looking elsewhere! But one technique of technical analysis that is worth examination is mean reversion.

Mean reversion is based on the mathematical premise that all prices eventually move back toward the mean or average. Thus, if a stock is underperforming, its price will move toward its average value when the market rebounds. On Betfair, if a horse has been trading at the same odds for a long period of time, you could say that the market has determined that price as the correct one for that horse. The theory of mean reversion suggests that following a short-term movement in the odds, the market shortly corrects itself back to that average.

Financial markets provide a good analogy to help you understand how the Betfair market works, but the analogy should not be taken too far. Although many people are using similar techniques to financial traders on Betfair, these techniques are not guaranteed to work in exactly the same way every time. Therefore, the advice remains the same throughout this book – if you're trying a new technique, 'paper-trade' it for a period of time first. If the technique is successful, by all means start trading for money, but again, keep stakes low at first. This cautious approach allows you to check whether a particular strategy has merits in the long-term.

Keeping One Eye on the Event

As with the financial markets, rumour and counter-rumour, and events both inside and outside the market, can affect the odds on Betfair.

For example, the odds available on the horses may be affected if heavy rain begins to fall at a racecourse. Some horses run well on rain-softened ground, others don't. When the rain starts, horses that are renowned as soft-ground performers begin to shorten in the market, whereas the firmer ground specialists begin to drift.

In another example, if a contestant in a TV talent contest contracts bronchitis, his odds will begin to lengthen no matter what.

Profiting from the patriots

Some time ago, a friend of mine happened upon a great trading strategy. He noticed that in the hours before an England football match, the odds on England winning always shortened. He decided that this was due to patriotic English fans realising that the match was shortly going to start and wanting to add their financial backing to the team.

So whenever a big England match approached, my friend backed England to win as early as possible – knowing that he could lay the team back at lower odds just before kick-off. The plan worked well until the occasion when three late injury announcements made the odds on England drift dramatically. Instead of trading out of his position for a loss, my friend decided to stand the bet. England lost.

The lesson? Lots of factors affect odds and if a market turns against you, get out of your position quickly – plenty of opportunities will arise in the future to get the money back!

The markets can also react to other factors. A popular newspaper writer or television presenter saying that they like a particular horse, can affect the market, as can a confident trainer appearing in a television interview.

The key point to remember is that lots of factors can affect the market on Betfair, and you need to be aware of them. If you back a horse believing that the odds are about to shorten, and in the meantime the horse throws its jockey off and goes walkabout, its odds drift – no matter what economic theory states that it won't! Far better to get out of your bet for a guaranteed loss than to risk your entire stake in the vain hope that the market might turn in your favour.

Chapter 9

Low-Risk Betting: Arbing

. . . .

In This Chapter

▶ Examining ways of betting where risk is minimised

▶ Arbing to guarantee a profit

. . . .

Raiders of the Lost Arb

Throughout this book, I emphasise the ways in which Betfair resembles the financial markets. Another example of this similarity is the practice of *arbitrage*. On Betfair, however, arbitrage is called *arbing*, and people doing it are called arbers.

Economics textbooks tell you that arbitrage is the practice of taking advantage of a state of imbalance between two or more markets, by simultaneously striking deals in those markets that exploit the imbalance.

In betting terms, arbing is when you guarantee yourself a risk-free position by backing a selection at a high odds while laying it at lower odds elsewhere.

You may notice that the definition is almost identical to the one for trading that we covered in Chapter 8. The principle is exactly the same as buying-low and selling-high, or vice versa. The only difference is that when arbing, you look to strike your bets simultaneously and in different markets, whereas with trading, you wait for an individual market to move in your favour, before placing your two bets at different times.

Betfair is used for two distinct types of arbing:

- Between Betfair and another bookmaker
- Between different Betfair markets

Arbing between Betfair and another bookmaker

Historically, the only easily available type of betting was the ability to back – bet that something would happen. In the 1980s, however, when spread betting began to take off, people could both back and lay (bet that something would not happen). Or as the spread betting companies called it, buy or sell.

With the emergence of Betfair in 2000, this ability to 'operate on both sides of the market' became ever more prevalent, and part and parcel of everyday betting for many people.

This innovation meant that for the first time arbing became something that you could do in sports betting, just as those clever chaps in the financial markets had been doing for years.

But enough of the history lesson. Here's a real example of how arbing works:

In the 2002 Soccer World Cup, England and Sweden were drawn in the same group. And as often happens in events where countries compete against each other, patriotism overcame good sense.

In this example, most English-based bookmakers offered England at odds of 10.0 to win the World Cup. These odds were much shorter than they should have been, but the bookmakers were not concerned. They knew that people would back the team anyway.

On Betfair, the odds were a bit better at around 13.0, but still reflected the fact that patriotic English fans were less interested in getting fair odds and more interested in adding financial support to their moral support.

In Sweden on the other hand, punters cared less about the English team, and so a Swedish bookmaker was offering England at odds of 17.0.

Many switched-on arbers used this situation to massive advantage. For example, say that an arber backs England with the Swedish bookmaker for £100 at 17.0 to win the competition. At the exact same instant, he lays England for £130 at 13.0 on Betfair.

If England won the tournament, the arber would win £1,600 from his first bet ((£100 × 17.0) − £100). He would also lose £1,560 from his second bet ((£130 × 13.0) − £130). The result is a net profit of £40.

If England lost the tournament (which is what happened), the arber would lose the £100 staked in the first bet, but would win the £130 staked in the second bet, making a net profit of £30 (see Table 9-1).

Table 9-1   Simultaneously backing and laying the same selection at different odds with different bookmakers can guarantee you a profit no matter who wins

Result of World Cup	1st bet. £100 backed at 17.0	2nd bet. £130 laid at 13.0	Net Profit (Loss)
England wins	Wins £1,600	Loses £1,560	**£40**
England loses	Loses £100	Wins £130	**£30**

Arbing between different Betfair markets

Just as you can arb between other bookmakers and Betfair, you can also arb between different Betfair markets.

Here's a soccer example. Betfair offers a number of different types of markets on most soccer matches. One of these is a Total Goals market, where you can bet on whether a game will have one goal or more, two goals or more, three goals or more, and so on. In another market, called Over/Under 2.5 Goals, you can bet on whether a game will have more than 2.5 goals, or less.

Arbers: a very different animal

Most people bet for the enjoyment. Betting adds a little bit of spice to the event you're watching. If you happen to win some money as well, even better. If not, at least you enjoyed the event and got some excitement from it.

Arbers are a different kind of animal altogether. One day I got a call from the Betfair Helpdesk, who had an irate German customer on the phone. The Helpdesk couldn't understand his complaint and asked if I would speak to him.

The customer in question had spotted an arbing opportunity the previous day on a cricket match that was about to start and took it – he backed a team with another Internet bookmaker, and simultaneously laid the team on Betfair. He wanted to know why his bet hadn't been settled. Were Betfair incompetent? What were we up to? Did we care about our customers at all?

The problem was that the German customer knew nothing about cricket – he simply saw an arbing opportunity and took it. He didn't realise that he was betting on a five day test match – a match that still had four days left to play!

When this was explained to him, the customer said that he thought the situation was ridiculous: What kind of sport has a match that takes five days to complete? I said that I understood his frustrations, but that he should probably take up this particular complaint with someone else. An example, if it were needed, that being a successful arber doesn't necessarily require any sporting knowledge!

You may have already worked out that backing that a game will have three goals or more is exactly the same as backing that the game will have over 2.5 goals. Therefore, on occasion, you can take advantage of arbing opportunities between these two markets.

Say you notice that in the Total Goals market, 3 goals or more is available to back at 3.5. In the Over/Under market, over 2.5 goals is available to lay at 3.4.

So, you back 3 goals or more for £1,000 at 3.5 and simultaneously lay over 2.5 goals for £1,030 at 3.4. If 3 goals or more are scored in the game, you win £2,500 from your first bet ((£1,000 × 3.5) – £1,000) and lose £2,472 from your second bet ((£1,030 × 3.4) – £1,030). The result is a net profit of £28.

If less than 3 goals are scored in the game, you lose the £1,000 staked in the first bet, but win the £1,030 staked in the second bet, making a net profit of £30 (see Table 9-2).

Table 9-2	Arbing opportunities also exist between different Betfair markets		
Number of goals in game	*1st bet. £1,000 backed at 3.5 – Total Goals Market*	*2nd bet. £1,030 laid at 3.4 – Over / Under Market*	*Net Profit (Loss)*
3 or more	Wins £2,500	Loses £2,472	**£28**
Less than 3	Loses £1,000	Wins £1,030	**£30**

Some Final Words on Arbing

A few years ago, arbing opportunities presented themselves quite regularly on Betfair and in the betting market as a whole. Unfortunately, a good thing can't be kept secret for long. Lots more people are arbing now, and they're becoming ever more sophisticated.

We have rules for this

Arbers were out in force for the Nissan Open golf tournament in February 2005. A friend of mine was happily backing golfers to win the tournament with a fixed-odds bookmaker and then laying them back with Betfair whenever he saw a mistake in the odds. Things were going especially well – he couldn't believe how many 'mistakes' the fixed-odds guys were making.

During the 3rd round of play, after the leaders had completed about 50 holes, torrential rain arrived, and after much debate, the tournament was abandoned. Not to worry, thought my friend – it's a shame if bets are voided (meaning all stakes are returned), but no harm done. If bets are honoured, great – after all, an arb is an arb.

Unfortunately, it turned out that the fixed-odd bookmaker had a rule stating that any tournament in which 36 holes had been played would be deemed to be completed. So all my friend's bets on (losing) golfers were settled as losers.

Betfair, on the other hand, had a rule that 54 holes must be completed for a result to stand, so all his lay bets on the same golfers were simply voided.

He lost around £900, but says to this day that he learned a valuable lesson – make sure you understand the rules of any market before getting involved.

Some bettors are even using *bots* (see Chapter 10 for a full explanation of bots) that automatically read betting markets and bet accordingly when an arbing opportunity exists.

More people arbing in more sophisticated ways, means that finding opportunities for mere mortals to arb is increasing difficult. But that doesn't mean that opportunities never exist – you just need to be quick enough to take advantage of them.

I refer to arbing as low-risk betting, not no-risk betting – and the distinction is critical. No-risk betting doesn't exist. Although arbing gets pretty close, the biggest risk is always time. Arbing is all about placing two bets almost simultaneously. The reality, of course, is that this is not always possible, and if the market moves in the split-second between bets being placed, you can sometimes miss the arbing opportunity and be left with a position you don't want.

Chapter 10

Automating Your Betting

• •

In This Chapter

▶ Introducing bots

▶ Looking at different types of bots

▶ Examining some different bot strategies

▶ Getting started with bots

• •

*B*etting is likely to take up a fairly small amount of your time. For most people, betting is an interesting diversion from the rest of life, a diversion that provides a bit of fun from time to time.

But if you decide to go for a far more labour intensive betting strategy, at some point you'll need to ask yourself whether some or all of your activity can be automated. The answer is yes.

This chapter gives you a brief introduction to automating your bets and points you in the direction of further information.

Becoming Familiar with Different Types of Bots

Robots, commonly known as *bots*, allow people to automate their betting. Bots are automated betting programs that your computer runs on your behalf, based on a series of conditions that you provide.

Betting bots, just like other robots, are used to perform repetitive and complex tasks that are more difficult or time consuming for a human.

I'm not a programmer, so I can't tell you about the technical ins and outs of different bots, but I can give you a brief outline of the two main types: API bots and screen-scraping bots.

If you get to a stage where you want to build a bot, a programmer can advise you whether an API or screen-scraping solution is best for you.

API bots

API stands for Application Programmers Interface. The API allows people to build bots and have them communicate directly with Betfair's database. So instead of you clicking something on the Web site, which then communicates with the database and sends a message back to the Web site for you to see, your computer talks directly to Betfair's computer to retrieve data, and place and manage bets.

Programs in a number of common programming languages can use API. Therefore, if you or those helping you have programming experience, writing a bot that does what you want is relatively straightforward.

Screen-scraping bots

A less sophisticated (but not necessarily worse) option is to use a *screen-scraping bot*. This option means that your computer draws data from Betfair by 'reading' the screen in much the same way as a person.

The bot can then interpret the data, and based on a number of programmed conditions, submit and manage bets through the Web site.

Using a Bot

Don't think that automating your betting automatically means a guaranteed profit.

A bot is only as good as the conditions with which you program it. Automation of a poor strategy simply means that you lose money, just much more efficiently and quickly than before!

Test any strategy manually until you are certain you can obtain the right results. And after the bot is built and in operation, keep stakes small at first so that you can closely monitor the results the bot is achieving and refine where necessary.

Expect to make a number of changes to your bot in the early stages of monitoring. The first version built rarely works perfectly, and some bot users I know are on their fourth or fifth full version. They are constantly making improvements and alterations as the markets in which they operate change.

Planning your bot use

Varying degrees of automation can be employed with your betting – from using a bot to speed up a single aspect of your betting to using one that takes over every aspect of your end-to-end betting process. (The really clever bots may even bring you breakfast in bed!)

For example, if you specialise in in-play betting, you may become frustrated at how long it takes you to place your bets using the standard Betfair interface. You can build (or have built) a bot that allows you to click one button to back or lay automatically a selection with pre-defined odds and stake.

This type of bot is relatively simple. A human is still required to pre-define the stake and odds, make a selection, and instigate any bet. All the bot does in this instance is speed up the process of submitting a bet – a slow and cumbersome process for a person to do.

A more complex bot is one that assesses where the weight of money is in a market. This type of bot automatically makes bets in those markets, with the intention of trading out of those positions when the odds moves in a particular direction (for a full explanation of trading, see Chapter 8).

In this instance, your involvement can be limited to choosing the markets that the bot can trade in and setting the parameters under which it can do so.

Employing different bot strategies

Many people assume that bots are useful only for automating the lower risk betting strategies, such as trading and arbing (see Chapters 8 and 9).

Bots are tremendously useful if you plan to employ these kinds of strategies because much of the work involved is repetitive and requires fast calculations – ideal territory for a bot.

However, you can also employ a bot for more traditional forms of betting, such as finding value bets. In this section, I outline two examples where bots can be used in both lower risk and more traditional types of betting.

Employing a bot to arb

You can use a bot to exploit arbing opportunities in the final of a darts tournament. Betfair usually runs an outright market on the overall winner of a tournament. It also runs individual markets on the winner of a particular match. Obviously, by the time the tournament reaches the final, two different, yet identical, markets exist – a final match market and the outright tournament market.

You can build a bot that constantly monitors both of these markets, and whenever one market is out of sync with the other (that is, you can lay one player at lower odds in one market than you can back them at in the other market), the bot automatically places the necessary bets to guarantee you a profit.

In most cases, a bot is likely to be much more successful than a person employing this strategy manually. A bot is quicker at constantly navigating between two different markets, spotting odd discrepancies, and working out and placing the necessary bets.

Employing a bot to find value bets

Say that you have a ratings system to assess the relative ability of participants in your chosen sport. For example, you may track lower league soccer teams by recording all their past performances and assigning a numerical value to each team.

When two soccer teams meet, you compare the ratings that they have achieved historically and work out the varying percentage chances of each team winning or the result being a draw. You convert these percentages into odds and look at the market on Betfair. If any of the available odds are bigger than your estimate, you place a back bet of £50. (I explain value bets in full in Chapter 6).

You can automate this entire process. Although speed isn't such a pre-requisite in this example, using a bot to analyse and place bets in this fashion allows you to reduce your workload and potentially increase the amount of games you can analyse.

If your ratings are good, the increased amount of bets lead to faster profits. If, on the other hand, the ratings aren't so good, a bot helps you realise it quicker!

Being aware of the risks of bot use

The advantages of using bots are clear, but one of the key disadvantages is that you are potentially giving up some control and an element of human sense-checking on what the bot is doing.

Before using a bot, try to think through all the exceptional circumstances in which your bot may not function effectively.

For example, how is your bot going to cope with non-runners in a horse-race? And what about the unlikely event of a tie in one day cricket, or a tennis match where a player gets injured and looks like she's going to retire hurt?

All of these circumstances are unusual and can affect betting markets in strange ways. If your bot is unaware of them, it can cost you a lot of money. You need to ensure that you've considered all the instances where something unusual may happen, and that you have a plan in place to deal with these problems.

Obviously, a well-built bot can theoretically take into account all instances where something might go awry and deal with the situation effectively, but you may want to build in safeguards that alert you when something out of the ordinary is occurring.

At the end of the day, the key to winning on Betfair with a bot is the same as with human betting. Have a strategy, and stick to it. Start small, monitor how things go, and refine as necessary.

Buying or Building a Bot

Several third-party applications are already available, and these bots can do most of the things that people commonly want to automate.

But if a bot that does what you want isn't already available, you can build it yourself or have it built for you. Building a basic bot can cost as little as a few hundred pounds. A very sophisticated bot can cost as much as you're prepared to pay – especially if you want it to make you breakfast in bed!

Whichever route you choose, the ideal starting point is Betfair's Developers Program http://bdp.betfair.com, shown in Figure 10-1.

Figure 10-1: The Betfair Developers Program Homepage.

At this site, you can find a list of commercially available bots, and also a list of established programmers with experience of working on Betfair projects. An area also exists where you can post your bot specifications and invite bids from programmers to build it for you.

Chapter 11

Going Pro

● ●

In This Chapter

▶ Deciding whether you've got what it takes

▶ Making the decision to become a professional gambler

▶ Setting yourself up

▶ Following a professional punter during his working week

● ●

*P*rofessional gamblers have always existed, but the revolutionary nature of Betfair gives them a better chance to bet efficiently and effectively.

Going professional is still not a decision to take lightly, though. Being a professional gambler may seem glamorous, but you're not just giving up one job for another: your new one has probably got a lot more risk and uncertainty associated with it.

Although I'm not a professional gambler, I work and have contact with a number of professionals through my job. Therefore, this chapter is largely my observations on the qualities that these people share.

Professional gambling is not for everyone. In this chapter, I cover what you need to have in place to turn professional, some of the skills and attributes that are required to make a living betting, and how Betfair can give you an edge in that. And I share a week in the life of a professional gambler.

Working Out What Constitutes a Living

Ask yourself how much money you want to earn from gambling in a year. Do you just want to replicate your current salary? Do you want more? Are you happy with less?

Now, work out what you need to win in a month and in a week. From your experience of betting, does this amount sound reasonable?

I can't give any guidance on coming up with a salary goal; that must be your call. But you have to be honest with yourself: £10,000 a week may be a bit too much to aim for!

Assessing Your Qualities

Not everyone has the qualities required to be a professional gambler. They are a rare breed. First, you need to be able to cope with the relative solitude of the job. Second, you have to be able to cope with the uncertainty.

And then you have to be good enough to make consistent profits. The following sections outline the most common attributes of successful professional gamblers.

Being analytical

Every professional gambler I've ever met – in fact every winning gambler I've ever met – shares this one trait: they are analytical about their gambling.

You never hear professional gamblers say something like 'I think it's about time so and so won a match, and so I'm going to back him'. Instead, professionals minutely analyse an event and come to a conclusion as to the percentage chance of something happening.

And some of them use very in-depth methods to do so, such as spreadsheets, databases, and automated programs. Professionals feel able to make a valid decision on whether to bet only when they have all the information.

Specialising

Losing gamblers bet on too many different things. Glance at the profit and loss account of a losing gambler and you often see bets being placed on everything from horse-racing to golf to financial markets to reality TV and so on.

To win consistently, you have to specialise. The degree to which you do so depends largely on your personality and style of betting, but you need to be realistic about your capacity to follow enough events closely enough to be able to bet successfully on them.

A friend of mine bets only on two-year-old horses running on the flat. He bets on nothing else, ever. He claims that only by having a finite and defined population of horses can he possibly know everything he needs to know about them. As a result, he rarely has more than three or four races a day that fall within his betting strategy. And he doesn't bet at all between November and March, because of the limited racing for two year olds.

I know other professional gamblers with a much wider scope – snooker, cricket, and lower-league English football, for example. But however narrowly or widely they specialise, they all know, and don't stray from, the limits of, their knowledge.

Having discipline

Imagine sitting down for an hour to analyse a tennis tournament using a ratings system that helps you assess the relative abilities of tennis players. You put hours of work into this system and it indicates that Roger Federer is the most likely winner, with about a 70 per cent chance of winning. You carefully examine the draw and see no causes for concern. He has excellent head-to-head records against his likely opponents in the early rounds, his recent form on the surface is excellent, and you see no reason why he's not going to win.

Then you look at the betting, and he is 1.4 to back. There's no value in backing him – your ratings system says he has a 70 per cent chance of winning the tournament, and his odds on Betfair reflect that chance almost exactly. (I explain percentage chances and odds in detail in Chapter 6.) Do you have the discipline to walk away after putting in all that work?

People who lose money are often ill-disciplined. They place bets just for interest, make bets based on opinion rather than analysis, and chase any losses they incur.

Without the discipline to stick to your long-term strategy no matter what is happening, you will eventually lose.

Working hard

All the professional gamblers I know work at least a standard working week. And most work a lot more. Add to that the extra stress and solitude of working on your own, and it becomes clear that professional gambling is much more than throwing a bit of money around for a few minutes a day.

If you aren't prepared to put in the hours, the chances are that you won't win in the long run.

Taking the Plunge

If you do want to make betting your living, and feel that you have the skills to make it work (see preceding section), plan to have a trial period where you test your strategies.

A few evenings a week or the odd weekend for a few months can suffice. This experiment allows you to refine your strategies and work through the problems you're bound to encounter.

Working through teething problems with computers, satellite reception, or your office set-up, is best done when you're not relying on gambling to pay the mortgage!

The time to make the move is when everything is in order and you feel confident.

If possible, having a back-up plan is a great idea. Perhaps working part-time, or perhaps making sure your old job will take you back if things don't work out. Obviously, finding a job of some description is easier if you have a highly transferable skill, such as computer programming or accountancy.

Diary of a Pro Punter

A professional gambler who uses Betfair (as well as other betting companies) agreed to let me sit next to him for a week while he talked me through what he had done and what he was doing.

He specialises mostly in horse-racing, but also bets on a number of other events. He employs a number of different profitable strategies – backing, laying, in-play betting, trading, and arbing – so his activity gives a good idea of the range of ways you can try to make money on Betfair.

Although this diary is not a verbatim record, I took plenty of notes to ensure that it represents a good summary of what he said. He may use some phrases that are new to you, but they're covered in the various sections of this book if you wish to look back at them. (See the Glossary, or look them up in the Index.)

Day 1

Today should be a good one. There's some great horse-racing at Cheltenham, and they're at the final stages of the World Darts championships – two televised events that always create a lot of activity on Betfair.

I spend the morning updating the speed ratings I keep for horse-racing. I track the times that horses run for every race in the UK and Ireland and create a speed rating for each performance. I use this to quickly assess the relative ability of horses when analysing a race to see if there are any value bets.

I then get stuck into analysing that day's racing. I tend to focus on a particular type of race at this time of year that are termed novice hurdles – it's important to specialise in this way, because it's the only way you can keep track of everything that's going on.

A horse called Denman is very interesting in the first race at Cheltenham. He ran a fast time in his first race for an inexperienced horse, and I decide that he would represent a value back bet at any odds bigger than 4.0. But on checking the price, I see that he's only available at 3.9. So it's a no-bet. It's difficult to not bet when you've done all the analysis – but it's the key to long-term profits. If the horse isn't value, then it's not value – so leave it alone.

In the same race, there's a horse called Its A Dream. He's joint favourite at around the 4.0 mark, but his form is nowhere near as good as Denman's, and on my speed ratings, I reckon he should be more around the odds of 10.0. I'm fairly sure that the only reason he is such short odds is that his trainer and jockey are popular and their horses often get over-hyped. But I'm more interested in fact than hype, so I put in a lay of £100 at 3.9 and am pretty confident that it will get matched. It does.

I look at all the other races and analyse a few in detail – but all the prices look about right to me and I don't see any value bets. But that's okay, the hard work always pays off in the long run.

A bit of lunch and then the first race is off. Denman absolutely slaughters the field and looks to be a pretty special horse in the making. I'd be lying if I said I wasn't frustrated that I haven't backed him, but you have to get over those feelings – it wasn't a value bet at the time, so forget about it. Regretting not having a bet is a losing mentality in the long run. And anyway, Its A Dream came nowhere so I won £100 on the race.

The big race of the day involves a horse called The Listener who has been impressive in his two runs to date this season. He's trading at around the 1.85 mark. Whenever you have a short priced favourite like this it's always a good opportunity to trade, because the majority of the money in the market centres around the one horse – people either want to back it or lay it. So in the last 15 minutes before the off I start trading – laying at 1.83, backing at 1.85, and on and on. It's not exciting, but if you can predict the way the market is moving, it's a very easy way to make money for little risk. I manage to lock in a £63 profit, so no matter what happens in the race I'll win.

I watch the rest of the day's racing, but no opportunities to bet come up, except for a horse that doesn't jump the first couple of fences too well in one of the later races. I try to put in a lay, but some other people beat me to it, so I cancel the bet and forget about it. The horse actually gets its jumping together and almost wins the race, so I feel glad that I missed the bet originally because it would have been a nervous few minutes!

The darts starts at 7 p.m., so I've got a couple of hours off. Drag myself to the gym. Staring at a computer screen all day isn't all that great for the body and getting out and doing something is crucial – not that I'm very good at motivating myself to do it!

Back for the darts. I've been noticing throughout the tournament that another bookmaker has been slow to update its prices in the handicap match betting markets. Very often a player will win a set and yet it will take the bookmaker a good minute to adjust their price.

The same happens tonight and I'm able consistently to back players with the fixed-odds firm and almost immediately lay the same player at a lower price on Betfair. You notice these arbing opportunities from time to time and have to take advantage – because it doesn't take long for the fixed-odds guys to cotton on to what is happening. I've had more accounts closed by these guys than I've had hot dinners!

But tonight it all goes well and I make £186.

£349 profit on the day.

Day 2

I wake early and see that Kicking King, the favourite for The Gold Cup, one of the big races of the year, has been ruled out for the season with an injury. A number of horses have been backed to win the race as a result of his absence and their prices have shortened. But people seem to have forgotten about a horse called L'Ami who has been performing well in the top races and isn't that far behind the quality needed to win the race.

He's 37.0 in Betfair's antepost market for the race so I back him for £200. I'm fairly sure that the market will come round to his chances in a few days and I'll then be able to lay off my stake at lower odds and lock-in a profit. That's the theory at least!

All that analysis of the Gold Cup means I'm behind on my work for the day. I update my speed ratings as quickly as possible and then start looking at the day's racing. One horse interests me and is 14.0 on Betfair. I reckon it should be no bigger than 5.0 so back it for £200. It falls at the first fence – ouch!

There are three short-odds favourites on the card today, so I spend a boring hour trading on the three of them. I backed one of them for £300 at 3.2 as the money on the lay side was starting to build up and it looked like the odds would shorten. But then his trainer was interviewed on TV and said that he didn't rate the chances of the horse, and so the money disappeared and his odds began to drift. I get out of it the best I can by laying him back at 3.5 for £274. It's a guaranteed £25 loss but better than £300!

It's always better with trading to accept a small loss and move on. Waiting for a market to turn in your favour can be dangerous and lead to a much bigger loss. And anyway, I make £162 trading on the other two races.

Racing is over and my attentions turn to a cricket test match in Pakistan. I spent a lot of time looking at some statistics last year and it is obvious that international test matches have become much more aggressive, meaning that matches are less likely to end in a draw these days. I lay the draw for £1,000 at 2.2 with the intention of backing it at 2.5 when the match goes in-play. All I need is a couple of wickets to fall early and that'll easily happen.

More darts tonight, but some others have obviously cottoned-on to this arbing trick. It's become much more difficult to lay off my stake on Betfair and after a couple of hours I call it a day, with only £18 to show for my darts efforts.

£45 loss on the day.

Day 3

Wake up at 4 a.m. The test match in Pakistan starts at 4:30 a.m. and I need to be ready to get my back bet in on the draw as quickly as possible after it goes in-play. The match starts and I put up an unmatched back bet of £900 on the draw at odds of 2.5. This means that if it gets matched I will be guaranteed to win £150 if it's a draw or win £100 if anything else happens.

I go back to bed at 4:45 a.m. and dream of batting collapses. Back at the computer at 9 a.m. and the bet is matched after five quick wickets fall early on.

Update my speed ratings, but there's no racing today in the UK and nothing of interest in Ireland, so today is for catch up.

I've been working with a programmer to try to automate how I create my speed ratings, and he comes at lunchtime to discuss progress. Five hours on and although he is confident, I'm not sure whether it's going to work. I like the manual side to how I do things because it means that I can check and double check every figure to make sure it's accurate. Not sure I can trust a computer, but then it would save me about three hours a day!

No money made or lost on the day and a 6 p.m. finish – and that's on a day off!

Day 4

Up at 6 a.m. today. I'd been hoping to work on a new snooker ratings system that I've been building yesterday, but didn't get the chance because the programmer was here too long.

It's based on what's known as an Elo ratings system, something that they use to rank serious chess players. The basis is that all professional snooker players start off with a virtual 1,000 points. Whenever they play each other, they put a number of these points at risk, say 50. Whoever wins takes all the points, meaning they now have 1,050. This goes on and on. It's a way of assessing the relative ability of players and a good starting point for any snooker betting.

There are a couple of big tournaments on the way and having watched the snooker markets on Betfair for a while I'm sure that there's money to be made. But I'm pretty sure that I'll only 'paper-trade' for the rest of this season to ensure that the ratings are up to scratch. I've dived into betting before too early and lost money. Just because you've put lots of time into developing a ratings system, doesn't mean it will work!

I analyse the day's racing. There's one horse that stands out. I reckon he should be a 3.0 shot, but he's currently available at 11.5. I put up a small back bet at 12.5 with the intention of topping this up over the course of the morning. By the start of racing I've managed to get £300 matched. I could have put all the money up at once, but that could have affected the market, pushing the price of the horse down, so it's worth trickling it in when you have the time.

There's an early race with an odds-on favourite that I trade for a bit and make £43 on the race.

Then the horse I'd backed in the morning runs and wins for a £3,450 profit. I'd be lying if I didn't say I was feeling pretty pleased with myself, but it's best to be as detached as possible. It was a value bet and it happened to win, but lots of other value bets lose. It's the long-term profit you have to focus on.

The World Championship darts is over, but another world title (for a different governing body) starts in a few days. I'll be keeping an eye out for arbing angles in the early rounds and then probably get involved in the final stages.

Lots of high profile soccer matches on tonight, but to be honest, I've never been able to make soccer pay. I know that lots of people can, but I've just never found an angle – despite investing hours in analysis and losing money trying out different approaches. That's just the way it is really – you are good at some things and bad at others and you just have to specialise. Soccer's not for me, so it's a 6.00 p.m. finish.

£3,493 profit on the day.

Day 5

Strange day today. Up at 7 a.m. and complete my speed ratings for the previous day's racing and then analyse the afternoon's fare.

There are five bets today that look like value. That's a lot for one day. Can't work out whether I'm just looking at them differently because I had a big win yesterday or whether they really are all value bets.

I decide to be cautious and decide on two of them that I will back. I'll leave the other three alone. Best to be cautious.

The two I back lose and the other three win. That's made me mad. I tied myself up in knots this morning second-guessing myself. In retrospect they were all value bets – sometimes there are five in one day – and I should have backed them all. Now I've lost £600 when I should have made another £800 or so.

I need to compose myself – it's no good betting angry! I was planning to trade on a tennis match tonight but I'll call it a day there at 4:30 p.m.

I feel tired as well. People think that being a professional gambler is easy. I don't think they realise the hours of work I put in. Maybe I need a holiday.

£600 loss on the day.

Day 6

Sleep in late today – which isn't a good idea when there is so much to get done before racing starts – but feel that I really needed it. I'm at my desk by 11 a.m. and feel like I'm in a much better frame of mind now.

There are no value back bets today, but there is an interesting novice chase with two joint favourites at around 2.5. The market seems to have forgotten the rest of the field and I'm not sure why. The two favourites are the odds they are only because they represent the two most powerful stables in the country – not because their form warrants it.

I lay them both – something I call a 'double take-on' – for £200 at combined odds of 1.25. I don't think the two of them have a combined chance of 80 per cent of winning so I'm happy to lay them.

They both fall on the first circuit and a 90.0 shot wins the race: £200 won.

No other bets for the day, but I'll be keeping an eye on the rest of the racing from Sandown Park. They've had a lot of rain there recently and the ground is very testing. And the final half-mile is all uphill. I think there may be a number of horses which are leading at the bottom of the hill that will trade at an artificially short price in-play and then tire before the end.

It's hard to say exactly what I look for when betting in-play – which doesn't sound very analytical! But over the years I've watched enough races to know when a horse has gone too fast early on. And just like humans, if they run too fast too early, they won't finish well.

And that's the thing about being analytical. It doesn't have to be all spreadsheets and databases, as long as you're taking a methodical approach and basing your assumptions on knowledge.

It's not until the last race of the day that an opportunity arises. Two horses went off far too quick and one of them is left in the lead with 400 yards to run and looks like he'll go on to win. But I'm convinced he'll tire and get passed. I lay £555 at 1.1 (it's quicker to type in 555 than 500 and speed counts in-play!). The horse tires dramatically and ends up coming fifth.

That's racing over for the day.

The horse I backed in the Gold Cup, L'Ami, has now shortened in price and I think about laying my stake off. But to be honest, I still think he represents value and so I'm prepared to leave it for the time being. If it reaches anywhere near 14.0 I might change my mind.

£755 profit on the day.

Day 7

Racing is abandoned today due to frost and so it will be a quiet day. There's a tennis tournament on in Australia that I'll trade on in-play, but other than that I'll be focusing on finishing my snooker model. It's been four months in the making now and I'm excited to see how it works out.

The tennis is a disaster. It's a tournament in Australia and I'm convinced there must be people with at least a ten second advantage over me with the TV pictures I'm receiving. I lay a player for £2,000 at 1.91 thinking I'll be able to almost immediately back him back at 1.92. Then suddenly the price collapses and he's only available to back at 1.76. Something must have happened that I haven't seen yet.

I toy with taking the risk to see if I get matched at 1.92 eventually, but then sense prevails. I back him at 1.76 to guarantee a loss of around £170.

In the next point the other player falls and twists his ankle. A few people obviously got those pictures before me and that's why the prices changed so quickly. I'm glad I got out of the position as it doesn't take the guy long to finish his injured opponent off.

Enough of this – I can't bet in-play with that kind of information disadvantage.

The cricket match I bet on earlier in the week has finished with a Pakistan win, so at least I bag £100 profit from that.

In the evening I toy with the idea of having a bet in the eviction market of a TV talent competition. A friend was telling me that in every show in the last three years, the evictee has been one of the first four people to sing. The favourite to be evicted is singing last and I think of laying him. But hang on, I don't know enough about this stuff. I'll leave it alone.

£70 loss on the day.

End of week report

£3,882 up for the week.

That's a very good week, quite a bit up on the average. Last year I made £88,000 in total, but then you need to take £20,000 off that in costs (a programmer I use, satellite subscriptions, broadband, a new computer, and so on).

People always look at me suspiciously when I say I'm a professional gambler. I think they expect something altogether different – not a bespectacled geek who likes spreadsheets!

But analysis and hard work are the key to making money and I'm just not convinced that you can be profitable without it.

It's hard work. This week I've been sat in front of my computer for over 60 hours, I've only gone to the gym once and I've hardly spoken to my wife. I'm earning more now than I did working in IT, but I'm not convinced I'm better off overall.

My best advice for someone thinking of going pro is to work at it while you've got a job to make sure that you can make it pay. Have trial days on the weekend and when you do start full-time, make sure you have something to fall back on if it doesn't work out. It's not for everyone, so there's no shame in admitting that to yourself. As much as I would like to be a brain surgeon, I just know it's not going to happen.

And don't be any under illusions. It can be very solitary. If you enjoy the social side of work then you will have to work out a way of retaining that somehow.

Other than that, all I would say is good luck!

Chapter 12

Problem Gambling

1 started gambling at a very young age – I can't recall exactly when, but certainly younger than the law allowed. In one form or another, I've been involved in gambling ever since, and now I earn my living at it. If my mother holds any faint hope of me changing jobs and becoming a doctor or priest, she probably needs to accept that the die is cast.

Gambling is great fun, and plays a constructive role in most gambler's lives by providing a diversion from life's worries.

However, for some gamblers, the harmless diversion can turn into something more serious. And when it does, the effects can be devastating. Financial difficulties, relationship breakups, and psychological problems are just some of the common results.

Problem gambling and gambling addiction can have many of the same adverse consequences as other addictions, such as alcoholism. The particular problem with gambling is the difficulty others have in spotting the addiction. People notice if someone's always drunk or stoned – but how do you tell if someone has just lost his next mortgage payment.

 If you're reading this chapter and thinking that none of this applies to you, that's great. But even if that is the case, this chapter is still worth reading, because much of what the problem gambler does is what the winning gambler doesn't do. These are the things you need to avoid to win on Betfair.

In this chapter, I look at how to stop gambling ever becoming a problem, how to tell whether you may be struggling, and where you can turn for assistance.

Preventing a Problem

Most Betfair customers, at one time or another, display characteristics associated with problem gambling.

This fact doesn't mean that all Betfair customers have a gambling problem – far from it! Long-term profits, however, rely on gamblers being analytical and disciplined, and as humans, we occasionally fall short on both these counts.

At one time or another, most people have bet on an event 'just for interest'. Very little thought goes into the bet, and although people occasionally win like this, most of the time they lose in the long run.

Similarly, a lot of people lose money on one bet and immediately look for another bet to 'recover the losses'. Most people realise that this strategy is flawed and manage to refrain. Others place the bet and succeed in their aim. What's certain is that although you will sometimes be successful in 'chasing' (as this behaviour is known), at some point, losses become so large that nothing is left to chase them with.

Betfair has a number of tools to prevent you from replicating these types of mistakes.

I recommend that even the most disciplined individual sets up some of the following limits, however confident he is that he'll never stray from his strategy or common sense. This extra level of discipline doesn't cost anything!

To place some parameters around your betting, do the following:

1. **Log into your account on Betfair.**

2. **Click My Account at the top of the screen.**

3. **Click My Profile on the left-hand side.**

   On this screen you see a section with Responsible Gambling next to it.

4. **Click Edit.**

   This process brings you to an area where you can manage three aspects of your account to assist with problem gambling (see Figure 12-1):

1. **Limit currency deposits.**

   This setting allows you to set a maximum amount to deposit into your account in a time period. For example, you may decide that you don't want to deposit more than £100 a month into your Betfair account. This limit prevents you from chasing losses, because you can't deposit the money required to recover what you've just lost.

2. Limit losses.

Here you can set a maximum amount of money to risk in a time period. Once you have lost this amount, the system stops you from placing any more bets.

3. Exclude me from the site.

If things get very bad, this option allows you to close your account for a period of time.

Figure 12-1: Betfair allows you to set rules around your betting activity.

If you feel that you're having problems managing your betting, Betfair staff are trained by Gamcare, an organisation in the UK that helps problem gamblers. They can advise you of different ways to manage your account and point you in the direction of further help.

Recognising a Problem

Recognising that you may have a gambling problem is difficult. Reaching the stage where you fully admit the problem and seek help, is even harder.

If you are beginning to question whether your gambling is becoming something more than a controlled activity, try answering the following questions. If you answer 'yes' to a lot of them, seek help:

1. **Is gambling affecting your home life, work life, or relationships in general?**

2. **Do you feel guilt or remorse when you gamble, or afterwards?**

3. **Do you have a strong urge to continue gambling no matter whether you win or lose?**

4. **Has gambling adversely affected your financial position?**

5. **Have you been feeling down, depressed, or not your usual self?**

Just because you answer 'yes' to one of these questions doesn't mean you are a gambling addict. Plenty of us feel depressed on a Monday morning, without having a gambling problem! But do ask yourself the preceding questions once in a while as a quick check on your activity.

Getting Help

Several people I know admitted to having a gambling problem and sought help, and they all tell me the same thing – stopping made them happier.

Admitting that you're struggling with something can dent anyone's pride, but the results are cathartic. You no longer have to try and hide all your feelings and live in a world of semi-secrecy. Instead, you can talk about how you're feeling and be honest with people.

Friends and families are a key source of help for many problem gamblers, but professional organisations in different countries can offer support and counselling as well.

Organisations vary by country. Within the UK, Gamblers Anonymous and Gamcare both work with people with gambling problems.

If you're outside the UK, enter 'gambling addiction' on an Internet search engine to find a local organisation that can help. If this fails, call Betfair's Helpdesk for assistance.

A friend of mine, who used to have a gambling problem, has three things to tell anyone struggling with gambling addiction:

- ✔ You're not alone
- ✔ You can find a way out
- ✔ You can find people to help you

Part IV
The Part of Tens

The 5th Wave   By Rich Tennant

"I was aware of the Betfair account, but the pompoms are new."

In this part . . .

*E*very *For Dummies* book contains a Part of Tens. Here you'll find ten common mistakes that you should be aware of when betting, ten top tips for betting with Betfair, ten (or so) of the most interesting Betfair markets that have occurred and ten firsts achieved by Betfair.

Chapter 13

Ten Common Mistakes

• •

In This Chapter

▶ Avoiding some of the common pitfalls of using Betfair

• •

*W*henever I talk to Betfair customers about their betting, the subject of mistakes and mishaps always comes up. Everyone has a story to tell about losing money after making an avoidable error.

The surprising fact is that beginners rarely make these mistakes. Instead, the culprits are people who have been using Betfair for some time. Perhaps a misplaced sense of confidence is to blame, or perhaps people are trying to do things too quickly.

Whatever the reason, the purpose of this chapter is to make sure that you don't make the same mistakes.

Not Reading the Rules

Throughout this book I talk about the necessity of understanding both what you are betting on and the rules governing that bet.

Before you place any bet, make sure you look at the Rules tab on the right-hand side of the market. What constitutes a white Christmas? What happens in the event of a dead heat? Will unmatched bets be cancelled when an event goes in-play? You need to be able to answer this type of question to bet effectively. And if you are ever in doubt, don't bet.

Laying the Wrong Odds

My most embarrassing, but more importantly my most expensive, mistake on Betfair was the time I intended to lay a horse at 1.32 but unfortunately forgot the all-important decimal point.

The result was that I asked to lay a horse at 132! Luckily for me, enough money was queued up to back the horse and I only laid in at average odds of around 3.5. Nonetheless, a costly mistake – especially as the horse won easily.

Laying When You Mean to Back

At times, Betfair is all about split second decisions and fast fingers – grabbing those value odds of 3.0 before they disappear and the best available is 1.7. An equally common mistake to laying the wrong odds, is to lay when you mean to back. You can avoid both of these mistakes by taking a little extra time.

A useful function on Betfair is the Market View Settings, which you can find by clicking Settings at the top left-hand corner of any market. Using this screen you can change the colour of the Lay column to make it clearly distinguishable from the Back side of the market. I set up my account so it always displays the Lay side as a luminous yellow and this seems to have eliminated mistakes caused by mixing up the two columns.

No one knows how many people make this mistake and how often, but everyday, when reviewing odds movements over time for a particular selection, you can see spikes where odds suddenly gets matched at way above the going market rate. Although a bettor might just have a particularly strong opinion, the more likely reason is that someone is mistakenly laying rather than backing.

So take your time!

Taking the Available Odds in Quiet Markets

When markets first open on Betfair, some time can pass before enough people become involved to make these markets liquid (meaning there's lots of activity in them). Therefore, you often get people asking for unrealistic odds, and large spreads can appear between the best odds available to back and the best odds available to lay.

Even if you're in a hurry, don't be tempted to just accept the best odds on offer. If you do, in the long run you're consistently likely to accept worse odds than you should.

If you want to back a selection that is currently available at 2.0 to back and 3.0 to lay, you're much better off requesting a back of, say, 2.6 and waiting to see if it gets matched. If it doesn't get matched, you can always reduce the odds you're asking for at a later date.

This approach requires more effort, but in the long run your Betfair activities are more profitable.

Betting 'Just for Interest'

At one time, this book was called *Betfair For Dummies*. Had it stayed that way, I wouldn't have included this common mistake. However, the title now has *Winning* at the start, which means that I need to address this error.

Winning on Betfair (and in fact winning at gambling in general) requires the discipline to bet only when you've done the work and know that the odds you are backing or laying represent good value (for a full explanation of value, see Chapter 6).

Chasing Your Losses

You can easily get frustrated when your betting doesn't go to plan. Even the most disciplined of gamblers can tell stories about trying to 'fire their way out of trouble'.

A friend of mine worked on a soccer ratings system for several months and after lots of waiting, began to bet on what the ratings told him. Things started well – his first nine bets won and he was showing a healthy profit.

Then his tenth bet lost. He should have expected this to happen because no rating system is perfect: the important thing was to ensure that he made money in the long run. But my friend didn't like the fact that he'd backed a loser, and he started trying to recover his lost stake.

He proceeded to place various bets on greyhound racing, snooker, tennis, and golf (all sports that he knew absolutely nothing about). And instead of recovering his lost stake, he found his entire betting bank wiped out.

The lesson is: if you have a plan, stick to it. Long-term profits can be achieved only by having a consistent and disciplined approach.

Assuming Something Goes In-Play

Some betting strategies depend on taking a position (backing or laying a chosen runner or team) before an event starts and trading out of that position when betting goes in-play.

For example, if you think that an unpredictable wicket is going to make a cricket test match fairly volatile, you can lay the draw safe in the knowledge that you can back it later at a higher odds.

However, as with other similar approaches, this strategy is reliant on an event going in-play.

Although lots of events are covered in-play by Betfair, this is not always the case. So make sure you check the Rules tab on the right-hand side of the market before embarking on this kind of strategy.

Leaving Unmatched Bets Open

A good strategy can be to request bigger odds than are currently available, but you need to choose the markets carefully.

Ask yourself whether something could happen in a market that would see your bet being quickly matched with little chance of it winning.

For example, if you request to back that a contestant will be eliminated in a reality TV show, your bet could get matched after the contestant is ruled out of elimination for some reason.

So always think about what you are betting on. You need to decide when to leave unmatched bets on Betfair, and in what markets to do so.

Betting on Something In-Play That Isn't Live

In the Rules section for any in-play market, Betfair always display the phrase, 'Users should be aware that transmissions described as live by some broadcasters may actually be delayed'.

Always be aware that someone could have a few seconds advantage over you in the event you're watching on TV. For example, someone watching the US Masters from the 18th hole at Augusta knows that a golfer has sunk a putt before you do. Nothing is sinister about this, but the fact is that a few seconds can easily pass while the TV pictures you're watching go through production and bounce off different satellites.

Betfair puts a delay on placing bets in most in-play markets to protect customers, but still be aware about how fast your information might be.

Spending Too Much Time on Betfair

Betting on Betfair is fun, exciting, and provides intellectual stimulation – and if you do things right, you can make money. But you should be aware of how much time you spend betting.

Long-term profits come from selective betting; and by definition, if you're spending too long on Betfair, you probably aren't being selective enough.

It's obviously impossible to define how long is too long because it depends what kind of betting you are doing. But as a guide, you should plan how much time you are likely to be on Betfair for each day. If you are frequently spending longer than this, or betting on things that you hadn't thought you'd be betting on at the start of the day, then it's time to log off.

And if you find it difficult to log off, it might be worth checking out Chapter 12.

Chapter 14

Ten Top Tips

In This Chapter

▶ Taking advantage of some advice from Betfair customers

Discovering new things about Betfair can be difficult. Betting is something you typically do on your own, and so you don't usually have people around to ask for advice. I only began to discover some tricks and techniques to improve my betting, after I started working at Betfair and was surrounded by lots of other bettors.

For this list of top tips, I asked a thousand or so Betfair customers what helped them win on Betfair. This chapter outlines their most popular pieces of advice.

Have a Betting Bank

Put aside a designated amount of money for betting. Ensure that this amount is money that you can afford to lose if things go wrong. Ask yourself whether you have a maximum sum you're prepared to lose in a month or in a year. Whatever you decide, stick to it.

This advice may sound overly sensible and boring, but is vital if you're to make long-term profits on Betfair. If the money you allocate for betting is the same money you intend to use for mortgage payments or school fees, you're adding a whole new sense of pressure to the situation.

Undue pressure adversely affects your decision-making processes. Successful bettors are able to walk away after their tenth losing bet in a row because they know that their strategy will prove profitable in the long run. If you need a winning bet to pay the rent, you're likely to start doing things that aren't part of your long-term strategy. And that usually means you end up losing more money.

I know a professional gambler with an interesting outlook on this philosophy: 'I forget about the money completely. I do what I know will prove right in the long run and just use my betting bank as a way of keeping score. At the end of the year, if the bank is bigger than it was at the start, then I know that I was doing things right. If it isn't, then I know that I need to improve.'

It's also worth having regular reviews (say every three months) of your betting bank and deciding in advance what your approach to profits will be. If you are in profit, will you take the profit out and use it for something else? Or will you leave it in and look to increase your stakes accordingly? Both approaches have merits and your decision will be based largely on your attitude to risk. What's critical is that you make a decision in advance about what your policy will be and stick to it.

Although remaining detached from the money can be difficult, keeping a clear mind when betting ensures that the decisions you make aren't clouded by an overpowering need to win.

Assess Your Position with Market View Settings

Unless you're a walking calculator, quickly assessing your position in a market after making a bet can sometimes be difficult. Luckily, Betfair can do this calculation for you.

To access your position quickly:

1. **Log in and navigate to the market you want to bet on.**

2. **Click the link Settings at the top left of the market. The Market View Settings screen will appear.**

3. **Select and save a market profile that will make your betting a lot easier. Do this by checking the boxes for the options you are interested in.**

Here are the various options you can consider when working with the market settings:

✔ Change the colours of the Back and Lay columns. A more contrasting market view is a great way to prevent you accidentally laying something you mean to back. (See Chapter 5 for more on backing and laying.)

✔ Include settled bets in P&L figures. (See Chapter 3 for more on P&L: profit and loss.) In certain markets, such as the World Cup Winners market, once a country is eliminated, bets are settled on that country. Select this option if you want your overall P&L figures for that market to include bets that have already been settled.

> ✔ Show P&L figures net of commission. This option ensures that your current commission rate is included in any calculations.
>
> ✔ Show a separate future position. If you select this option every time you're about to make a bet, the screen shows what your position would be if you were to go through with the bet.

Try My Markets

The ability to bet on lots of different events, and choose from a multitude of different markets for each event, is one of Betfair's great advantages. This level of choice ensures that every style of betting is accommodated.

However, this large number of markets means that navigating to the things you're actually interested in can often take some time.

Fortunately, the My Markets link (on the left-hand side of the screen) allows you to select which markets you want to appear in the menu when you're logged in.

Open Multiple Betfair Screens

If you're betting on more than one market at the same time, open as many Internet screens as you want and log in to Betfair on each one. Then you can quickly navigate between the different screens instead of having to find each market in the menu.

Be Confident Enough to Back Drifters

In horse-racing, a lot is made of horses whose odds lengthen markedly before the race. Many people believe that any horse 'drifting' in the betting is as good as a certain loser.

But remember that a horse drifts because the majority of bettors thinks the odds are too short in the first place, and the market may often overreact.

A Betfair study looked at a sample of 65,000 horses competing in 2005.

Nineteen per cent of the horses that drifted significantly in the betting went on to win. This result is only slightly less than the 22 per cent of horses whose odds had shortened dramatically in the betting. Most importantly, if you'd placed £10 on all the horses, you'd have lost over £3,000 on the horses that had shortened in the betting and yet won over £2,000 on the drifters.

Therefore, if you think that a horse is a good bet, don't be afraid to back it just because it drifts in the betting.

Use Keyboard Shortcuts

Keyboard shortcuts can speed things up when you're trying to place a bet quickly.

Use the up and down cursor keys to adjust the odds you're betting at. You can also use the Enter key to submit your bets.

Redeem Coupons

Betfair provides coupons on certain events, and these allow you to view, and bet on, a range of different markets at once.

If you're interested in betting on a number of matches in the World Snooker Championships for example, using a coupon means you don't have to constantly navigate between the different markets.

Check Your Bet

Every time you submit a bet, Betfair takes you to a confirmation screen. When you first start betting on Betfair, check through the bet details on this screen to ensure that you're doing what you want to do.

As you become more confident, you can uncheck the Verify Bets option at the bottom of the Place Bets panel. But I don't advise making this change until you feel that you have a full grasp of what you're doing. Speed is important in some instances, but placing the bet you want is important all the time (see Beware Fat Fingered Typing below).

Experiment with the % Book Function

The bottom right corner of the Place Bets panel contains a box called '% Book'. Simply select this option to display the combined percentage odds at which you're either backing or laying.

This function is very useful when you're trying to work out the combined percentage chance of all your bets. For a full explanation of having more than one bet in a market and what the percentages mean, see Chapter 6.

Beware Fat Fingered Typing

In the world of financial markets, there is a syndrome called 'fat finger typing'. It manifests itself when a financial trader types incorrect details into their computer and executes a trade that they didn't intend. These mistakes happen on a daily basis, but in some cases the results are catastrophic.

In December 2005, a trader at Mizuho Securities wanted to sell one share in a new telecoms company at 600,000 yen. Unfortunately, he actually sold 600,000 shares at one yen each!

The mistake cost the company around 30 billion yen and sent panic through the Japanese financial markets, with the Nikkei 225 falling 2% on the day. And the trader who was guilty of the error is probably not all that popular with his colleagues. The Christmas party, scheduled for the day after the mistaken trade, and the payment of a staff Christmas bonus were both cancelled.

Although yet to be seen on Betfair to the same costly extent, it is certain that similar mistakes are being made by customers on a daily basis.

Talking to one customer who uses Betfair extensively on a day-to-day basis, he said, 'I spend a lot of time monitoring the markets through the type of betting I do and it is clear that from time to time, people make the most almighty errors. You'll suddenly see the odds plummet to far shorter than they should be or sky-rocket out to far longer. It's clearly someone who has backed when they meant to lay, or typed the wrong odds or stake in.'

Chapter 15

Ten (or So) Most Amazing Markets

A week rarely goes by without a Betfair market throwing up a surprising story – a 'certainty' that gets beaten, a huge odds turnaround for a particular selection, or a surprise win for an outsider.

The eclectic nature of Betfair makes selecting a list of the 'most amazing markets' hugely subjective. However, in this chapter I provide some of my favourite stories (more than ten because I just couldn't narrow them down!). These markets are illuminating and confirm that sport and life are unpredictable, the seemingly impossible can happen, and we should always expect the unexpected – especially when we're betting.

Cheltenham Gold Cup, Ante-post Market, March 2005

Kicking King had long been prominent in the ante-post betting for jump racing's blue riband, but after his trainer, Tom Taaffe, revealed that the horse had returned a 'dirty scope' (meaning that he had a respiratory infection) and would be unlikely to run in the Gold Cup, his odds drifted markedly – out to the maximum of 1,000.

Unfortunately for one layer, the horse staged a remarkable recovery, lined-up on the day of the race as a warm favourite, and proceeded to win the race easily.

In perhaps the most remarkable ante-post market story, one punter won nearly £25,000 for a £25 bet, and another won nearly £10,000 for £10.

Inter Milan versus Sampdoria, Match Odds Market, January 2005

Usually, if a soccer team is 2 – 0 down in the 88th minute of a match, the result seems pretty inevitable. Indeed, when Inter Milan were in this position, they were traded at the maximum Betfair odds of 1,000.

However, two minutes and three goals later, Inter Milan were celebrating a famous victory while one Betfair customer nursed severe bruises (and a five-figure loss) after laying what he thought to be an impossible result.

Final Ashes Test, Richie's Last Words Market, September 2005

The stage was set for a pulsating last day of play in the final test of the Ashes, with England needing a draw to regain the trophy. The day was also notable for marking the retirement from British broadcasting of Richie Benaud, cricketing and commentating legend.

On a Betfair market that asked customers to predict Richie's last words in the commentary box, 'Thank you', 'Goodbye', and 'It's been a privilege' were all backed heavily.

But, always the consummate professional, Richie simply handed over to his two colleagues, Mark Nicholas and Tony Greig, and so 'Name of anyone on the commentary team' emerged as the winner – traded at 24.0.

Next Newcastle Manager Market, September 2004

Next manager markets are notoriously volatile – with rumour and counter-rumour fuelling dramatic market swings. Perhaps the most volatile was the market to predict the next manager of Newcastle United at the start of the 2004/05 English Premiership soccer season.

Eventual winner, Graeme Souness, was matched at the maximum Betfair odds of 1,000, but maybe more remarkable were the number of different names supported as favourite over the course of the market.

Terry Venables traded at 1.45, Alan Shearer at 2.8, David O'Leary at 2.8, Steve Bruce at 3.75, Gordan Strachan at 4.0, and Steve McClaren at 4.0. Therefore, seven different individuals were favourite to get the job at one point or another.

Breeders' Cup Turf, Win Market, October 2003

One of the most exciting horse-races in living memory led to one of the most amazing in-play markets in Betfair history.

The European horse High Chaparral fought out a close finish with America's Johar, with both horses appearing to cross the line simultaneously.

Betfair's in-play market was left open to allow people to bet on the result of the photo finish – something that is usually confirmed in no more than a minute or so.

But this finish was very close. Because the race was one of the most important of the year, the judge wanted to make sure that he got it right, and it was over 15 minutes before he declared that the result was a dead heat!

During that time, over £250,000 was matched on the result of the photo finish.

Benson & Hedges Masters Snooker, White versus Ebdon, February 2003

When Peter Ebdon took a 5 – 1 lead in his match against Jimmy White, plenty of people thought the result was in the bag. Over £14,000 was matched on Ebdon at 1.01 (to win £140!).

Unfortunately, those Betfair customers who thought the fat lady was already in full flight, discovered that she was just warming-up. Jimmy White staged a remarkable recovery to win 6 – 5.

Champions League Final, Liverpool versus AC Milan, May 2005

At the start of the final, many Betfair customers thought that a draw in 90 minutes was a distinct possibility, and this result was backed at 3.2. However, few could have predicted the circumstances in which the draw came about.

Three AC Milan goals in the first half saw the draw trade out to an odds of 100. But three second-half goals from Liverpool secured the draw for a few lucky customers.

In the Champions League outright market, Liverpool traded at a high of 250 to win the competition before going on to claim the title 3 – 2 on penalties.

Ascot, Historic Place, February 2004

Some Betfair occurrences defy explanation – none more so than the in-play betting on the horse Historic Place after he had already passed the post first at Ascot.

The in-play market had been reopened after a stewards' enquiry was called to investigate whether Historic Place had caused interference to the runner-up, Senor Sedona, in the final stages of the race.

One Betfair customer must have had a strong opinion that the stewards were going to disqualify Historic Place because he laid £3 at 1,000 and £15 at 550 on the horse.

After some deliberation by the stewards, the result was left unchanged, costing the luckless layer over £10,000.

Debate still surrounds why the customer struck the bet. Betfair spokesperson, Tony Calvin, said at the time, 'It's a remarkable figure to be laid. Someone either had a strong opinion or it was a bet made in error.'

U17 World Championship Soccer, Cameroon versus Portugal, Match Odds Market, August 2003

One Betfair customer celebrated an unlikely result after backing the draw at 550 when Cameroon were 5 – 0 down against opponents Portugal.

Cameroon scored five goals – the last in the 92nd minute – to gain a bizarre draw.

Greyhound Derby, Heat 21, May 2004

Although, greyhound racing is a popular sport with Betfair customers, non-televised races rarely attract much interest.

So when someone requested a £1 million bet in the market on the greyhound Escholido, who was running in a heat of the Greyhound Derby at Wimbledon, people were amazed.

After all, a group of high staking bettors may sometimes trade £1 million on popular horses in the very biggest races, but rarely a single individual. And in greyhound racing, this size of bet is unheard of. Famed high-stakes punter Harry Findlay owned the greyhound, but he refused to respond to speculation that he requested the bet.

Ultimately, just a few layers were prepared to take on a bet with that amount of confidence and only(!) £192,000 was matched on Escholido – who went on to win the race easily.

Next Liberian President Market, November 2005

It is now common for Betfair's political markets to create a lot of interest – from bettors and political commentators alike. In fact, in most circles, these markets are now seen as a much more reliable guide than any opinion poll as to what the likely result of an election or important vote will be.

In the Australian Federal Election of 2004, pollsters were calling the race neck and neck. And yet on Betfair, the Coalition Party was the overwhelming favourite. The Coalition went on to win in a landslide. A similar story occurred a month later in the US, where pollsters couldn't separate the Democrats and Republicans. Betfair customers could though, having George Bush as the overriding favourite to win. Which he did.

But sometimes, the markets on Betfair get things very wrong.

When Betfair opened a market on who would be the next Liberian President, it wasn't a market they expected to attract much interest! But as ex-Chelsea and AC Milan soccer star George Weah was running for the office, they soon began to be proved wrong.

The market created huge interest, particularly as many Betfair customers thought that Weah's fame made him a certainty for government. At one point during campaigning, Weah was backed at the minimum Betfair price of 1.01 to become the next president.

However, the backers were wide of the mark as the largely unconsidered Ellen 'Iron Lady' Johnson-Sirleaf went on to win with a margin of around 20% of the vote to become Africa's first elected female leader.

FA Cup, Manchester City versus Tottenham, Match Odds Market, February 2004

This soccer match seemed like a lost cause when Manchester City found themselves 3 – 0 down at half time, and with a player sent off.

The Betfair market agreed, with City matched at 400 to pull off an unlikely result and over £200,000 matched on Tottenham at 1.01 – the lowest odds available on Betfair.

However, City's ten men made one of the greatest come-backs in FA Cup history to win 4 – 3 and leave Betfair customers shocked – some happily, others less so.

Chapter 16

Ten Betfair Firsts

In This Chapter

▶ A few firsts from Betfair's short history

*B*etfair opened for business on Friday 9 June 2000, and was initially run from a small office in Russell Square in London.

For the first time, instead of having odds dictated to them by a bookmaker, customers were able to set their own odds and see if anyone disagreed with them.

Fearing extra competition in their market, traditional bookmakers reacted by calling Betfair pariahs, criminals, and vagabonds.

This disdain for the new kid on the block wasn't helped by Betfair's first marketing slogan, 'Revolutionising Betting' – something that the established bookmaking industry wasn't exactly keen on!

A lot has happened since then. Betfair is now accepted as an established part of the bookmaking industry, with over 500,000 registered customers, 100,000 of whom are active in any one month. Customers in 85 countries use the site, and 14 different languages are available. The Betfair database deals with over 1,000,000 transactions a day, and at peak times matches more than 12,000 bets a minute.

And many 'firsts' have happened along the way. . .

First Market

Betfair's first market was the Epsom Oaks, won by Love Divine on Friday 9 June 2000.

Twenty-two participants took part in that market – most of them sitting together in a small office at Betfair HQ. The amount matched on the market was £1,476, with 63 bets made.

On the 2005 Epsom Oaks, over 12,000 customers made 38,000 bets, matching over £2.7 million!

First £1 Million Market

On 11 February 2002, Tiger Woods won his second successive US Masters golf tournament, beating Retief Goosen by three shots and joining Jack Nicklaus and Nick Faldo as the only golfers to record back-to-back victories in the event.

Although I'm sure Tiger knew that his victory was making golf history, he was probably unaware that he was also playing a part in Betfair history.

The Betfair market on the winner of the Masters that year was the first with a turnover in excess of £1 million (£1.8 million). In the process, Tiger became the first ever £1 million selection, with over £1.1 million turned over on him alone.

These days, £1 million markets are common, occurring on a daily basis.

First Novelty Market

From time to time, Betfair like to offer a betting market that's a bit different from the normal 'who will win a tennis match?' They call them novelty markets.

The first novelty market offered by Betfair was called Sorry Saturday. England's football, rugby union, and cricket teams all had a fixture on the weekend of 17 June 2000, and the market asked customers to predict how many of the teams were going to lose.

The market turned out to be such a novelty that no one bet on it!

Novelty markets are now massively popular on Betfair, with thousands of customers betting on everything from weather predictions to the next contestant to be evicted from the latest reality TV show.

First 1.01 Loser

The first selection to be backed at the minimum Betfair odds of 1.01 and then get beaten occurred in the first week of October 2001 in the FTSE Weekly Up or Down Market.

On 11 September 2001, in the wake of the Al-Qaeda terrorist attacks on the United States, analysts and Betfair customers expected the FTSE to continue to decline in value. Early on in the week, 'Down' was backed at very short odds, including a few bets at 1.01.

However, the FTSE began to rally, largely led by media groups such as Pearson, Granada, and Carlton, as well as biotech firms like Celltech, and by the close of trade was 129.6 points up on the week.

In fact, the FTSE actually closed at 5036, 2.3 points above the opening value of the FTSE on the morning of the attacks.

First In-Play Market

The first event to go in-play on Betfair was The Embassy World Championship Snooker Quarter Final on 1 May 2001, between Matthew Stevens and Stephen Hendry.

Hendry, the pre-match favourite, was backed at around 1.78 to Stevens' 2.30. But Hendry's attempt to win an eighth world title was foiled, and he lost 13 – 5 to his younger opponent. Hendry was magnanimous, 'I've no complaints – I was out played in all departments by a better man on the day.'

Stevens went on to be beaten by John Higgins in the Semi Finals.

In-play has since become a Betfair by-word, offering customers the opportunity to bet on all kinds of events after they have started. Snooker in-play has progressed to the point where betting occurs on the winner of each frame of a match!

In-play betting is covered in Chapter 7.

First 1,000 Winner Pre-Race

The first horse to be backed at the maximum Betfair odds of 1,000 before the race (not in-play or in an ante-post market) and go on to win was Arctic Blue, in Chepstow's opening race of the season on 23 March 2005.

A total of £64 was matched at the maximum odds, and many layers were convinced that the horse had little chance of winning. After all, Arctic Blue had failed to finish any better than sixth place in 13 attempts, and his jockey was having only his fifth ride in a race.

Arctic Blue won convincingly, and was expected to perform well in the future. But unfortunately, at the time of going to press, he has not taken part in another race, presumably due to injury. But at least he always has a place in the Betfair history books!

First Telephone Bet

Betfair opened its Telbet service on 20 August 2001, allowing customers to call up a dedicated broker to place a bet on their behalf.

The first bet placed via this service was a £50 back at odds of 1.34 on the horse Harry Jake, running in the 5:15 p.m. Maiden Auction Stakes from Nottingham.

Harry Jake won, winning our first Telbet customer £17 – admittedly not a life changing amount, but a win is a win!

At the end of 2005, Telbet had taken nearly 3 million calls and placed 2.5 million bets.

First Exchange Game

In September 2005, Betfair launched its first exchange game, Exchange Poker.

Exchange Poker gives customers the opportunity to bet on any of four randomly generated poker hands, backing them if they think the hand is going to win, or laying them if they think the hand is going to lose. Therefore, unlike traditional poker, punters can profit from hands that they don't think are going to win. (For more on backing and laying, see Chapter 5.)

Exchange Blackjack followed Exchange Poker, and other games are promised.

First Betfair Customer

Betfair account number one is registered to New Zealander Dwayne Williams, a Betfair employee at the time. But employees don't count as customers!

The first non-Betfair person to sign-up was Nick Fox, with account number 12. Nick was a horse-racing journalist who was always keen to be on top of any new developments that would help his betting.

Following a link he found somewhere on the Internet ('to be honest, I can't remember where', he admits), Nick took the plunge, opened an account and hasn't looked back since.

'I would now say that around 75% of my betting activity is on Betfair. I tend to focus on in-play football betting and laying horses in races where I think their odds are shorter than they should be.'

First MOU

Betfair signed its first Memorandum of Understanding (MOU) with the British Jockey Club in June 2003. The agreement meant that for the first time, a betting organisation would share with a sports regulator, personal details of customer(s) whose betting activity might be a threat to the integrity of the sport.

By signing the agreement, Betfair had to require all its customers to forego confidentiality in those circumstances. Traditional bookmakers have generally claimed that they can never name names to a regulator because client confidentiality is paramount to their customers. However, only a handful of Betfair customers chose to close their Betfair accounts rather than accept the new terms.

The MOU has enabled Betfair to work closely with the Jockey Club and assist them with investigations they are undertaking. This first MOU has formed the template for a number of others that Betfair has signed, including with the International Cricket Council (ICC), the English Football Association (FA) and the Association of Tennis Professionals (ATP).

Appendix

Glossary

● ●

Account: You need an account with Betfair to be able to place a bet. To open an account, click Join Now on the Betfair Homepage at www.betfair.com.

Account Balance: The amount of money you have in your Betfair account.

Arbing: Backing something at high odds in one market and laying it at lower odds in another market to guarantee a profit. Arbing is often done between Betfair and other bookmakers. See Chapter 9.

Back: If you think something is going to win you back it. See Chapter 5.

Betfair Forum: The place to go to talk to other Betfair customers. Click 'Forum' on the Betfair Homepage to find out what people have to say.

Bot: An automated programme for placing bets on Betfair. See Chapter 10.

Commission: Betfair charges you a commission of between 2% and 5% on your net winning position in any market. For a full explanation of commission and how it works, check out Chapter 5.

Delays: When you're betting in-play, Betfair often inserts a timed delay from when you submit your bet to when it gets placed on the system. You can see the length of the delay in the Rules tab on any market. See Chapter 7.

Helpdesk: Your first point of call if you're struggling with something. Your local helpdesk number can be found on the Betfair Homepage.

In-play: In-play refers to any betting that you do after an event has started. Betfair signify that an event is in-play using a white tick on a green background. For more on in-play betting, see Chapter 7.

KYC: Know Your Customer. If you bet a lot of money through your account, Betfair will ask you to complete a Know Your Customer (KYC) check. This is to verify who you are and is very similar to the check that banks carry out on customers.

Lay: You lay something if you think it won't win. See Chapter 5.

Liability: The amount of money you stand to lose on a bet.

Market Base Rate (MBR): Every Betfair market has a base rate that is used as the basis to work out the commission that customers pay on that market. See Chapter 5.

Matched bet: When someone who wants to back something and someone wants to lay something and they are coupled together, you have a matched bet.

My Account: If you want to do anything on Betfair other than bet (such as changing your username, updating your address, or changing your credit-card details) the chances are you'll do it in My Account, which you can find at the top of any Betfair page. See Chapter 3 for tips on how to use My Account.

Odds: The rate at which any bet is calculated. Betfair uses decimal odds. To calculate your potential winnings (backer) or losses (layer), simply multiply your stake by the odds and then subtract your stake.

Paper trade: Simulated trading that betters use to practice bets (backs and lays) without actually entering into any monetary transactions.

Password: To keep your Betfair account safe, we insist on you entering a password to access it. Make sure you pick a password that no one else can guess.

Refer And Earn: If you like Betfair, then tell your friends about it – and get money for doing it. Check out the Refer And Earn section in My Account for some easy money.

Robot: See 'bot' and see Chapter 10.

Stake: The amount of money that a backer is risking on a bet

TAN: Your Telephone Account Number, located in the My Profile section of My Account. You need this number to place a bet through Telbet.

Telbet: Betfair's telephone betting service. Call a broker who will place a bet for you. See Chapter 5.

Trading: Backing something at high odds and laying it at lower odds (or vice versa) to guarantee a profit. See Chapter 8.

Unmatched bet: If Betfair can't find someone who wants to either back or lay the bet you're asking for, your bet remains unmatched. If the bet never gets matched, your stake will be returned to you.

Username: You need a unique name to log on to your account.

Value: Value is betting on something at better odds than it should be. It's the equivalent of getting a great deal in the January sales. It's the Holy Grail of betting. See Chapter 6 for a full explanation of value.

Void bet: If an event gets cancelled, bets are voided on that event.

Index

• *B* •

• *N* •

• *O* •